Early Praise for *Docker for Rails Developers*

With the avalanche of DevOps tools in use, this text has definitely cleared up the mystery. I've been waiting for a Docker book aimed at Rails projects, and I'm now convinced Docker is the way to go.

➤ **Nigel Lowry**
Company Director and Principal Consultant, Lemmata

Docker for Rails Developers is a wonderful book that allows you to jump in and start converting your existing apps to run in containers. It is well written, easy to follow, and makes you want to keep reading. I recommend this book for anyone with a little Rails experience who wants to get a jump start on using Docker.

➤ **Chris Johnson**
Operations Manager, healthfinch

With this book at my side, I was able to help my team move our largest, highest-revenue service into containers. This migration made disaster recovery much faster and more reliable, and made it possible to open a data center in a whole new market.

➤ **Erin Dees**
Lead Software Engineer, New Relic

This is much more than a how-to book, with the best technical writing I've seen recently. Isenberg's excellent guide provides clear and understandable explanations of how to solve Rails-specific Docker DevOps issues. This is the kind of thing I wish Docker had published a long time ago.

➤ **David L. Bean, PhD**
   Director of Data Science, PayClip, Inc.

Docker for Rails Developers is more than just a fantastic resource for Ruby and Rails developers looking to get up to speed with Docker. It's a great, no-frills guide for how to use the technology in practical, real-world situations, and I'd have no hesitation in recommending this to Python or Node developers either. I've been waiting since 2014 for a go-to book to hand to the Docker curious, and this might just be it.

➤ **Alexander Lynham**
   Owner, envoys.io

Docker for Rails Developers

Build, Ship, and Run Your Applications Everywhere

Rob Isenberg

The Pragmatic Bookshelf

Raleigh, North Carolina

Our Pragmatic books, screencasts, and audio books can help you and your team create better software and have more fun. Visit us at *https://pragprog.com*.

The team that produced this book includes:

Publisher: Andy Hunt
VP of Operations: Janet Furlow
Managing Editor: Susan Conant
Development Editor: Adaobi Obi Tulton
Copy Editor: Nicole Abramowitz
Indexing: Potomac Indexing, LLC
Layout: Gilson Graphics

For sales, volume licensing, and support, please contact *support@pragprog.com*.

For international rights, please contact *rights@pragprog.com*.

ISBN-13: 978-1-68050-273-2
Book version: P1.0—February 2019

Ruth. In hindsight, writing a book whilst having a baby and renovating a house probably wasn't the best idea—who knew? Thank you for your patience, love, and support. None of this would have been possible without you.

Sammy. I couldn't have imagined the joy and love you'd bring into our life. Be kind, be brave, and be willing to take risks in pursuit of your happiness and passions. I love you so much.

Mum and Dad. Thank you for everything.

Contents

Part II — Toward Production

Acknowledgements

Thanks to Adaobi, my editor at The Pragmatic Bookshelf, for her constant positivity and encouragement, as well as excellent editing feedback on the book to help make it as good as it can be. I will miss our updates and bonding over our mutual love of Gordon Ramsay.

I owe a great deal of thanks to the following people who gave up their valuable time to read and provide feedback on the book (a thousand apologies if I have left anyone out):

- John Paul Ashenfelter
- David L. Bean
- Erin Dees
- Chris Johnson
- David Landry
- Nigel Lowry
- Alex Lynham
- Lee Machin
- Rory McCune
- Noel Rappin
- Chris Thorn
- John Yeates

The book is immeasurably better as a result of their contributions.

I'd also like to thank everyone who purchased a beta copy of the book while it was still being written. In particular, I'd like to thank people who submitted errata during this process—your confusion, frustration, and pain have hopefully saved others from suffering the same fate.

Finally, a huge thank you to the entire Pragmatic Bookshelf team for taking on and supporting this title.

Introduction

If you love Ruby on Rails, you're going to love Docker. They are kindred spirits, born out of similar ideals.

For me, the allure of Rails was its Big Ideas: generators, migrations, testing as a first-class citizen, convention over configuration, multi-environment setups built in, live-code reloading. While, individually, these features may not have been new, the combination made Rails more than the sum of its parts: it gave us superpowers.

Docker is doing for DevOps what Rails did for web development. It too is packed with Big Ideas: a holistic view of your app (hint: your app is more than just your Rails code), containerization (lighter-weight, faster, and more efficient than VMs), software delivery that doesn't suck (for example, Ruby installs the first time you run a Ruby script), fault-tolerant clustering and scaling out of the box (spin up production-like clusters on your local machine), expert-level security features baked in (for example, automatic key rotation). The list goes on.

Docker is lowering the barrier to entry, making DevOps tasks that previously would have been unthinkable suddenly within our grasp. It gives us a *new* set of superpowers.

That said, Docker is not a panacea or a silver bullet to solve all your DevOps challenges. As with all technologies, there are trade-offs (I'll try to point these out as we go). However, despite the trade-offs, as you'll discover in this book, there is value in adopting Docker.

What Is Docker?

Docker, the technology, is a set of tools built around the idea of packaging and running software in small, sandboxed environments known as *containers* (we'll get to the nitty gritty of these in *What Is a Container?*, on page 6).

At a high level, Docker provides five capabilities:

- *Packaging.* The ability to package software into a reusable, shareable format known as *images*.

- *Distribution.* The ability to easily share packaged software (images) with other people and deploy it to different machines.

- *Runtime.* The ability to run, pause, restart, or stop packaged software in a reliable, repeatable way.

- *Infrastructure creation.* Creating virtual machines ready to run our Docker containers.

- *Orchestration and scaling.* Managing the release of software to a single Docker node or across an entire cluster.

Together, these five things combine to enable a new way of delivering and running software.

Why Use Docker?

To build a Rails app, we typically develop on our local machine. Rather than each team member manually maintaining their own local development environments, we can use Docker to provide a common, standardized environment. This saves on repeated effort and helps avoid many forms of the "works on my machine" issues that can waste hours.

Other benefits of using Docker for your development environment include:

- *A holistic view of your app.* Rails apps typically need a database and other external dependencies like Redis and Elasticsearch. With Docker, these dependencies are no longer an afterthought or "add-on" like in Heroku; they are described and managed as fundamental parts of your app.

- *Single-command app installation and setup.* Have you ever set up a Rails app on your machine and spent an excessive amount of time installing specific versions of its software dependencies? Docker's built-in delivery mechanism means that new team members can go from zero to a running app in minutes. No laborious, error-prone, manual setup steps here.

- *Easy version management of dependencies.* Want to make sure everything works before switching to a new version of Ruby or upgrading the database? No problem: running containers is cheap. Just change the image version and away you go.

- *Huge Docker ecosystem.* We frequently need to incorporate other technologies as part of our Rails apps: NGINX, Redis, Postgres, MySQL, Memcached, Elasticsearch, HAProxy, RabbitMQ, Node, and so on. All these and more are already packaged and ready to go with Docker.

- *Simulate production-like environments locally.* We know that how our Rails app performs in development isn't exactly the same as in production. With Docker, you can simulate production scenarios by running your app in multi-node, production-like environments on your local machine.

Docker can also help once you move beyond development. It provides a consistent interface, whether you're running locally, on a continuous integration (CI) server, or deploying to production. Once built, the same image is run at every stage of your continuous integration/delivery pipeline, giving us confidence that our tested application will perform the same in each environment.

If you need to manage and deploy to your own production infrastructure, there are further benefits:

- *Deployment standardization.* Docker provides a standard way of packaging and delivering applications: each part of your app is a container, and each app is a collection of containers. From a DevOps perspective, one Docker app is deployed and managed in the same way as any other.

- *Reliability and resiliency features built in.* Ever been woken at 3 a.m. by a cranky CEO because your app's gone kaput? Docker clusters are self-healing: if an instance dies, new copies of your app will be spawned on the remaining nodes.

- *Reducing infrastructure costs especially at scale.* Containers are much lighter-weight than virtual machines (VMs), allowing resources to be used more efficiently. They also let you scale up the number of containers on a single host rather than spinning up an entire new instance.

- *Room to grow.* If your app is (or becomes) wildly successful, it's good to know that Docker has been battle-tested at massive scale. Google Compute Engine, for example, is built on Docker containers, using Google's open source orchestration tool, Kubernetes.

Who Should Read This Book?

This book is for experienced Rails developers who want to learn how to use Docker. I'm going to assume, throughout the book, that you're proficient at using Rails; this will allow us to focus on learning and applying Docker.

This book doesn't aim to be a comprehensive manual on Docker: several other books serve that aim. Rather, this book is your field manual to *building Rails applications with Docker*. We'll cover the most useful commands and features that you'll need, and I'll refer you to reference material as needed.

If you're curious to discover how Docker can fit into your day-to-day workflow as a Rails developer, you've come to the right place.

What's in This Book?

In Part I, you'll learn everything you need to know about using Docker for local Rails development, including core concepts like containers and images. You'll build up real-world knowledge, step by step, through a series of practical tasks. We'll start with the basics—running a Ruby script and generating a new Rails project—before learning how to run our Rails app by building our own custom image.

We'll quickly move on to Compose, a higher-level Docker tool for declaratively describing an entire app, and how it all fits together. As you learn more, we'll gradually layer up services like a database and Redis. We'll cover how to set up and run your tests so that you're fully proficient at using Docker for Rails development.

In Part II, we'll explore the process of deploying and running an application in production. We'll start by giving you an overview of the production landscape—the tools, platforms, and technologies that can be used. Next, using Docker's own tools, we'll provision machines, create a cluster, and deploy our app. We'll also scale our app's resources to meet its changing needs.

How to Read This Book

Docker has a challenging learning curve. It's a vast tool and ecosystem, and there's a lot to understand. Hopefully this book will help—it's carefully structured to avoid introducing too many new things at once.

Each chapter builds on the one preceding it, so, especially if you're unfamiliar with Docker, I recommend reading the book in sequence to get the most benefit. Even if you have more Docker experience under your belt already, this is the recommended approach.

Docker IDs and Following Along Yourself

 Docker generates various unique IDs. When following the examples, it's important to remember that the IDs generated for you will be different from those shown in the output. Don't worry, though; I'll point this out where it's particularly relevant.

Which Operating Systems Are Supported?

Although Docker is supported on all major platforms (macOS, Windows, and Linux)—and we'll lead you through the process of installing it on these in *Installing Docker*, on page 3—there are some minor differences between the platforms, particularly around file permissions and networking.

For that reason, I've chosen Docker for Mac as the default platform in the examples and discussion, but I'll point out any differences between other platforms when they come up.

Some Linux/Unix Knowledge Is Recommended

 Even with Docker on Windows or Mac, there's no avoiding the need to understand some Linux basics. Docker evolved out of Linux kernel features, so explanations and examples often rely on Linux concepts and programs. I'm going to assume you have this knowledge already. If not, there are plenty of free resources online you can use to learn more or brush up if you need to.

Online Resources

You can find useful resources related to the book online,[1] including:

- The source code used throughout the book (you're free to use this in any way you'd like)

- An errata page, which lists corrections for the current edition

Let's get started!

---

1. http://pragprog.com/book/ridocker

Part I

Development

As developers, the bulk of our time is typically spent developing applications in our local environment.

In this section, you'll learn, step by step, how to begin using Docker as part of your local development workflow.

CHAPTER 1

A Brave New World

In this chapter, we're going to make sure that you're set up with a working version of Docker on your machine. This is important so you can actually try it out for yourself and follow along with the examples.

Next, we'll dive straight in and execute our first ever Docker command—running a basic Ruby script. However, rather than relying on a version of Ruby installed on your local machine, we'll be using one supplied by Docker.

You'll learn the fundamentals of how Docker works, including what *images* and *containers* are and why we need them. We'll cover the basic anatomy of docker run—probably the most central command to understanding Docker.

We'll also begin our journey of incorporating Docker into our development workflow by learning how to generate a new Rails project with nothing but Docker. This app will become the subject of our various tinkering and discovery throughout the rest of the book.

Installing Docker

Let's get you set up with Docker on your machine.

There's little benefit to me walking you through the installation process step by step: Docker's docs do a great job at this and will stay more up to date. I'll simply point you in the right direction.

We're going to be using the free, Community Edition (CE),[1] rather than the Enterprise Edition (EE).[2] Docker CE itself comes in two flavors: *Edge*, which contains the latest features being developed, and *Stable*, which is, well, more

---

1. https://www.docker.com/community-edition
2. https://www.docker.com/enterprise-edition

stable. Make sure to install the latter as we don't want any unexpected surprises getting in the way of your learning as you follow along with this book.

Go ahead and read the following instructions for your OS, then install Docker and meet me back here when you're done. Don't worry, I'll wait—there's nothing that floats my boat quite a like a brand-spanking-new Docker install.

macOS

Docker provides a downloadable installer called *Docker for Mac*, which has everything you need in one neat package (it's currently a 115.6 MB download). Go ahead and install this, following the installation instructions.[3]

Once installed, Docker for Mac adds a menu bar app in the top right of the screen featuring Docker's logo, which is its whale mascot affectionately named "Moby Dock." The menu bar not only tells you whether Docker is running, but it also provides other useful information and settings. You can find out more about the advanced settings available in docs.[4]

Linux

Unfortunately, getting started with Docker on Linux is a bit more involved than on other platforms. As you'd probably expect, how you install it depends on your Linux distribution.

Visit the Docker CE installation docs,[5] select your Linux distribution from the navigation menu, then follow the instructions. Typically, this involves installing Docker with your distro's package manager, which may need to get the latest packages from Docker's repository, as the distro packages are often outdated.

You'll also need to review Docker's post-installation instructions[6] to make sure you've got everything set up correctly. It will help you troubleshoot any issues you encounter.

In later chapters, we'll rely on a tool called *Docker Compose*, which, on Linux, is installed separately. Go ahead and install this using the documentation provided.[7] If you happen to have it installed already, I recommend upgrading to the latest, stable version.

---

3.   https://docs.docker.com/docker-for-mac/install/
4.   https://docs.docker.com/docker-for-mac/#preferences
5.   https://docs.docker.com/install/
6.   https://docs.docker.com/engine/installation/linux/linux-postinstall/
7.   https://docs.docker.com/compose/install/

Windows

How to install Docker depends on whether your system supports *Hyper-V*, Microsoft's homegrown virtualization technology. Professional, Enterprise, or Education editions (64-bit versions) of Windows 8 and up do have support for it—hardware permitting—but Windows Home edition, notably, does not.[8]

If your system supports Hyper-V, download the *Docker for Windows* installer,[9] launch it, and follow the instructions. Docker for Windows installs a widget in the Windows notification area at the bottom right of your screen (you may need to click to reveal it). Clicking the widget will open up a menu where you can find out more info and adjust various settings.[10]

If your system doesn't support Hyper-V, you will need to download and install Docker Toolbox,[11] a legacy way of running Docker on Windows.

Verifying Your Install

Let's check that Docker is installed and running correctly. Since Docker is a command-line tool, go ahead and crack open your favorite terminal, and enter the following command:

```
$ docker version
```

If all is well, you should see some output like the following:

```
Client: Docker Engine - Community
 Version:           18.09.0
 API version:       1.39
 Go version:        go1.10.4
 Git commit:        4d60db4
 Built:             Wed Nov  7 00:47:43 2018
 OS/Arch:           darwin/amd64
 Experimental:      false

Server: Docker Engine - Community
 Engine:
  Version:          18.09.0
  API version:      1.39 (minimum version 1.12)
  Go version:       go1.10.4
  Git commit:       4d60db4
  Built:            Wed Nov  7 00:55:00 2018
  OS/Arch:          linux/amd64
  Experimental:     false
```

---

8. https://docs.microsoft.com/en-us/virtualization/hyper-v-on-windows/reference/hyper-v-requirements
9. https://docs.docker.com/docker-for-windows/install/
10. https://docs.docker.com/docker-for-windows/#docker-settings
11. https://docs.docker.com/toolbox/toolbox_install_windows/

Don't worry if you have a newer version than shown here. You're all set.

Before We Begin

Got Docker installed? Great, you're just in time—I didn't want to start without you. Before we get our hands dirty and start playing with Docker, it's helpful to understand two fundamental concepts: *containers* and *images*.

What Is a Container?

Conceptually, a container is an isolated or "sandboxed" execution environment—an empty vessel for executing software in. Containers rely on virtualization features built in to the Linux (and more recently, Windows[12]) kernel, which let you create a fully isolated set of processes that don't know (or care) about the rest of the system. In fact, inside a container, it appears to be a complete Linux (or Windows) system, even though, in reality, all its resources and capabilities come from the host machine it's running on.

Containers can be started, paused, resumed, and stopped, leading many people to draw comparisons with virtual machines (VMs). In reality, though, aside from this similarity, containers are different beasts. Whereas VMs require a host OS, a software abstraction layer known as a hypervisor, and an entire OS installation for each instance, containers are very close to the metal. Each container is just piggybacking on the resources of a single kernel, with just a thin layer of isolation. This means you can run many more containers on a single machine than VMs—they're faster and use less resources.

What Is an Image?

As we just said, a container, in the abstract, is just an empty vessel for executing software in. To start a specific container, you need to supply it with some specific environment or context—what you'd need in order to run an NGINX web server in one container would be quite different from what you'd need to run, say, MySQL in another container.

The environment or context that you supply when you create the container—known as an *image*—is everything that makes the container unique. For example, what does the filesystem look like? What environment variables are set? What command is being run? So, an image is a bundled up package of everything needed to run a (specific) container.

---

12. https://docs.microsoft.com/en-us/virtualization/windowscontainers/about/

Using an image, you can spawn as many containers as you like that all look the same. For this reason, you may find it useful to think of an image as a *factory* for creating specific containers. People have also likened images to an abstract class in programming, and containers to instances of that class.

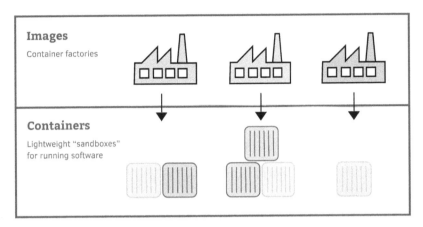

Images are ideal for sharing and distributing software: they use a standard format that is designed to be portable. Docker provides built-in tools for distributing images. By sharing images, you can collaborate on software development between your team and make your software available for deployment.

Running a Ruby Script Without Ruby Installed

We're about to perform some magic. Using Docker, we're going to run a Ruby application without needing Ruby installed on our system.

Have a look at this:

```
$ docker run ruby:2.6 ruby -e "puts :hello"
Unable to find image 'ruby:2.6' locally
2.6: Pulling from library/ruby
cd8eada9c7bb: Pull complete
c2677faec825: Pull complete
fcce419a96b1: Pull complete
045b51e26e75: Pull complete
3b969ad6f147: Pull complete
f2db762ad32e: Pull complete
708e57760f1b: Pull complete
06478b05a41b: Pull complete
Digest: sha256:ad724f6982b4a7c2d2a8a4ecb67267a1961a518029244ed943e2d448d6fb7
994
Status: Downloaded newer image for ruby:2.6
hello
```

Whoa. What just happened there?

If you look at the final line of output, you'll see the output we expected from our Ruby script: "hello". So somehow it worked. But how? Why?

The docker run command has the following format:

```
$ docker run [OPTIONS] <image> <command>
```

This command starts a new container based on <image>, and executes <command> inside the container. You may find it helpful to think about it in two parts: docker run [OPTIONS] <image> says what type of container we're going to run, whereas <command> says what we want to run inside the container.

So looking back at our command, we have:

❶ `docker run ruby:2.6`

❷ `ruby -e "puts :hello"`

The first part says that we want to run a container based on the ruby:2.6 image. As we said previously (*Before We Begin*, on page 6), an image is a bundled-up package of everything needed to run (a specific) container. The ruby:2.6 image is no exception; it has Ruby 2.6 preinstalled, with all its dependencies, allowing us to create containers capable of running this version of Ruby.

The second part of the command specifies *what* we want to run inside the container. In this case, we're saying we want to run the Ruby interpreter with a script passed in using the command-line option -e. The script is the most basic you can imagine: it simply outputs the word "hello".

Terminology: Running an Image

 We may occasionally talk of *running* an image, but strictly speaking, this is incorrect. Images can't be run directly; they are immutable factories for creating containers. Instead, what we mean is that we *create a container based on the image*, and it's the container that can be run.

Our docker run command will work on any machine that has Docker installed— even one without Ruby.

How is that possible? It's all very well that the image ruby:2.6 has Ruby installed, but how did we magically have it on our computer?

In actual fact, we didn't.

When we executed the docker run command, you may have noticed that it said Unable to find image 'ruby:2.6' locally. Docker then proceeded to download the ruby:2.6

image, which is why the command took a little while to run. Rather than download the image in one go, it downloaded the parts—known as *layers*—that make up the image. So Docker provides a seamless mechanism for delivering exactly the images we need, when we need them.

Why So Slow?

If you run the previous command yourself, there's one slight flaw you may notice: it takes a *looonnng* time. I know interpreted languages like Ruby are slow, but this is ridiculous.

The prior discussion helps to explain why the command took so long. The thing that took the time wasn't executing our tiny Ruby script; it was downloading the ruby:2.6 image over the network. Whenever you start a container based on an image that you haven't used before, Docker will need to download it first.

Although images are typically *much* smaller than VMs—MBs rather than GBs—waiting 20 seconds for every Docker command would be pretty frustrating. Thankfully, we don't have to. Docker stores downloaded images locally, so the next time you start a container based on the same image, it starts up at virtually native speed. Docker even caches *individual layers* of the image, allowing for reuse of layers between images, as we'll see shortly.

Let's see this for ourselves. Try running the same command for a second time.

```
$ docker run ruby:2.6 ruby -e "puts :hello"
hello
```

Wow. Much faster this time—no output about images being downloaded.

Cleaning Up After Ourselves

Each time we run the docker run command, Docker creates a *new* container to run the command. We've now run our Ruby script twice, so we have two virtually identical containers for running this Ruby script.

To list the running containers, we use:

```
$ docker ps
CONTAINER ID    IMAGE     COMMAND     CREATED     STATUS     PORTS     NAMES
```

As you can see, there are no running containers—that's because when our Ruby command terminated, the container running it also terminated. However, unless we tell it otherwise, Docker will keep this stopped container around in case we want to use it again.

Let's list *all* our containers, including stopped ones, by adding the -a option:

```
$ docker ps -a
CONTAINER ID   IMAGE       COMMAND     CREATED     STATUS      PORTS   NAMES
974e2bcb8266   ruby:2.6    "ruby …     1 seco…     Exited…             dazzling_ba…
7f8d7dddd6b5   ruby:2.6    "ruby …     3 seco…     Exited…             hungry_heis…
```

Here you can see two containers: one for each time we ran the Ruby command. However, we no longer have any need for them; we can delete them with:

```
$ docker rm <container id> [<container id2> ...]
```

Your container IDs will differ from mine as they are randomly generated. To delete these containers, I'd run:

```
$ docker rm 974e2bcb8266 7f8d7dddd6b5
```

However, you will need to substitute your container IDs to run this. Do this now to clean up your containers.

In the future, when creating a container we have no further use for, we can use the --rm option, which tells Docker to delete the container after it completes. The fancy word for short-lived containers that are deleted after they've served their purpose is *ephemeral*, but I prefer the word *throwaway*. Here's how we'd run our Ruby script in a throwaway container:

```
$ docker run --rm ruby:2.6 ruby -e "puts :hello"
```

This is a fairly common pattern, and you'll see it throughout the book.

Generating a New Rails App Without Ruby Installed

Running a Ruby script was cool, but what else can we do?

Wouldn't it be nice to start using Docker for some "real-world" tasks? Let's imagine we want to create a new Rails project (that's not so far-fetched…we are Ruby developers after all). Can we do that? You bet.

We're going to want to run multiple commands in succession in a container in order to generate the Rails project. We *could* craft a really long, ugly docker run that executes the instructions one after another. However, that's going to be hard to comprehend.

Instead, we can do something a little different. We can start a container running an interactive Bash shell. When we do this, we literally get a terminal session running *inside* the container. From there, we can run as many commands as we like, much like if we had a local Bash session. This is a very useful trick to have up your sleeve.

Let's give it a whirl.

Before we start, though, you'll need to find a directory on your machine where you want to generate the Rails project files. As our upcoming Docker commands will affect our local files (we'll cover exactly how shortly), I recommend that you create a new, empty folder where you'll run the steps from. For example:

```
$ mkdir ~/docker_for_rails_developers
$ cd ~/docker_for_rails_developers
```

All set? Great. We're now going to start an interactive Bash shell inside a container based on the now familiar ruby:2.6 image:

```
$ docker run -i -t --rm -v ${PWD}:/usr/src/app ruby:2.6 bash
```

You can see we're using the --rm option to create a throwaway container that will be deleted once we are done with it. There are also some new options (-i, -t, and -v ${PWD}:/usr/src/app) that we haven't seen before. We'll come back to these in a moment. For now, though, when you run this command, you should be greeted by a terminal prompt that looks something like this:

```
root@0c286e8bda42:/#
```

This different prompt shows that we're now successfully running a Bash shell *inside* a container. The root@ and # indicate that we're the root user—this is the default user inside a container.

From this new Bash prompt, we now can issue any commands we want the container to run. This begs the question...what do we want to run? Remember: we're trying to generate a new Rails project. So, first, let's move into the folder we're going to use for our project:

```
root@0c286e8bda42:/# cd /usr/src/app
```

Now let's install the Rails gem:

```
root@0c286e8bda42:/usr/src/app# gem install rails
```

Rails Version

The examples in this book have been built and tested against Rails 5.2.2—the latest version at the time of writing. However, except where we use new Rails features, everything should largely work for previous versions of Rails too.

You should see the Rails gem and all its dependencies being installed. This means we're now ready to generate our project:

```
root@0c286e8bda42:/usr/src/app# rails new myapp --skip-test --skip-bundle
```

We're using the --skip-test option to tell Rails not to use its default of Minitest. That's because in Chapter 7, we use RSpec to demonstrate how to configure our tests in a Dockerized environment.

We also use the --skip-bundle option. This tells Rails not to run bundle install after generating the project. The container is just a temporary vehicle for us to generate the Rails project—since we're going to get rid of it, there's no need to install the project dependencies.

When we run our rails new command, we get the following output, which shows our Rails project files being created, just as we'd expect:

```
create
create   README.md
create   Rakefile
create   .ruby-version
create   config.ru
create   .gitignore
create   Gemfile
«...»
create   vendor
create   vendor/.keep
create   storage
create   storage/.keep
create   tmp/storage
create   tmp/storage/.keep
remove   config/initializers/cors.rb
remove   config/initializers/new_framework_defaults_5_2.rb
```

Great! We can see our Rails files being generated. Remember, though, that we're *inside* the container, and we need to get the files onto our local machine. How do we do that?

First, let's terminate our Bash shell, which will stop the container:

```
root@0c286e8bda42:/usr/src/app# exit
```

This returns us to our familiar terminal prompt: $.

Now let's have a look inside the current directory on our local machine:

```
$ ls
myapp
$ cd myapp
$ ls
Gemfile      Rakefile     bin    config.ru   lib   package.json   storage
vendor       README.md    app    config      db    log            public
tmp
```

Huh. Somehow the files generated inside the container are here on our local filesystem. Aren't containers completely isolated? How did that happen?

The answer lies in the -v option we ignored in our docker run command. In Docker parlance, this *mounts a volume*—effectively sharing a portion of our local filesystem with the container. Specifically, -v ${PWD}:/usr/src/app says, "Mount our current directory inside the container at /usr/src/app" (${PWD} is a Unix environment variable pointing to the current directory). This means that any files in our local directory would be visible in /usr/src/app inside the container. Similarly, if we create, delete, or edit files in this container directory, the changes will be reflected on our local filesystem.

Here, mounting the local volume meant that the Rails project generated inside the container (within /usr/src/app) remained in our local directory, even after the container terminated. Additionally, this feature will be useful during development to allow us to edit files locally, and have the changes be picked up automatically inside the container, without having to rebuild the image.

It's worth noting a couple of key points about how this mounting behavior works. Firstly, if the /usr/src/app directory did not already exist inside the container, Docker would create it. Secondly, if the directory does exist inside the container, the mounted directory overlays and *masks* its contents while the mount is in effect.

Linux Users Only: Change File Ownership

 You'll notice that our newly generated Rails project files are owned by root. That's because, by default, containers run as root (UID 1). In order to modify the files, you'll need to change their owner:

```
$ sudo chown <your_user>:<your_group> -R myapp/
```

You'll have to do this whenever we generate files inside a container. For more details, see *File Ownership and Permissions*, on page 199.

Finally, we come to the -i and -t options. To understand these, we first have to understand Docker's architecture.

The heart of Docker—the Docker Engine—is a client-server application. The Docker CLI (the docker command) is just a thin client that tells a separate program—the Docker daemon—to do what we've asked. The daemon is responsible for doing the heavy lifting in terms of starting, stopping, and otherwise bossing around our containers.

The following figure shows the high-level architecture of Docker on Linux:

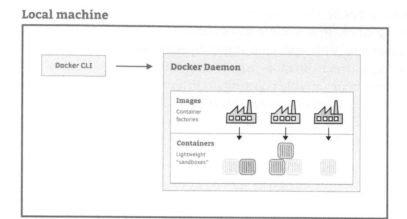

However, Docker is built on Linux containerization technologies that Mac and Windows do not have natively. Docker gets around this by installing a lightweight Linux virtual machine that runs the Docker daemon. This leads to a slightly different architecture for Docker for Mac/Windows, as shown in the following figure.

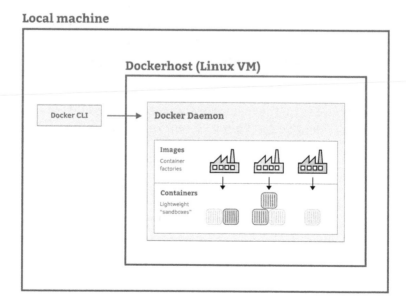

So how does this help us explain why we need to use -i and -t options?

Unix processes have three channels for I/O: standard input (stdin), standard output (stdout), and standard error (stderr). Since the Docker daemon runs in a separate process, Docker would have to actively do something to forward our CLI input to the Docker daemon.

By default, however, docker run only forwards the container's output to our client. That's fine when we want to run a container that requires no input. However, sometimes we run processes that do require input. An interactive Bash session is a great example of this—it waits to receive the commands we enter. In this case, we need to explicitly tell Docker to forward our CLI input on to the Docker daemon. We do this with the -i option—"i" for input. If we didn't specify this, the container would terminate immediately, because Bash—receiving no input —would terminate.

However, this alone is not enough. An interactive Bash session must be run inside a *terminal emulator*, which is responsible for things like displaying a prompt and interpreting escape sequences such as Ctrl-C. If we start a container to run bash, by default this runs in noninteractive mode, executing any commands provided, and terminating once it's done. To achieve a long-lived, interactive Bash session inside a Docker container, we have to tell Docker to set up a terminal emulator for us (technically a pseudoterminal or pty) that sits in front of Bash. We do this by specifying the -t option for docker run.

Now, if this all sounds quite complicated, just remember that whenever you need a long-lived, interactive session, you need to specify both the -i and -t options. In fact, these are commonly combined into the shorthand form -it, which you can think of as meaning "i"-n-"t"-eractive. Neat.

And with that, our work here is done.

Quick Recap

Now that you've had your first taste of Docker, let's pause for a moment to catch our breath and review what we've learned.

In this chapter:

1. We installed Docker on our machines.

2. We ran our first ever Docker command, a *helloworld* Ruby script, without needing Ruby installed on our machine.

    ```
    $ docker run ruby:2.6 ruby -e "puts :hello"
    ```

3. We saw how to list our running containers with docker ps and all containers (including stopped ones) with docker ps -a.

4. We deleted our old containers with docker rm <container id> and saw how to create throwaway containers using the docker run's --rm option.

5. We generated a new Rails project using a container by:

    • Starting an interactive Bash shell running inside a container

    ```
    $ docker run -i -t --rm -v ${PWD}:/usr/src/app ruby:2.6 bash
    ```

    • Installing the Rails gem inside the container

    ```
    root@0c286e8bda42:/usr/src/app# gem install rails
    ```

    • Using the freshly installed Rails gem to generate our project

    ```
    root@0c286e8bda42:/usr/src/app# rails new myapp --skip-test \
                                                --skip-bundle
    ```

Nice. We're well on our way to Docker proficiency. In the next chapter, we'll find out how to run our new Rails application.

## CHAPTER 2

Running a Rails App in a Container

By now you should be starting to become familiar with the concepts of Docker, like *images*, and running *containers* based on those images. Don't worry if you don't remember all the commands and various options. The most important thing is that you're beginning to understand the high-level concepts—all the rest will follow as you start to use Docker more and more.

In the last chapter, we created our shiny new Rails app. After the amazement began to wear off at how cool it was to generate an app with Ruby supplied by Docker, you were probably left pondering an important question: how the heck do I actually run it?

In this chapter, we're going to pick up where we left off to get our new app up and running. So, have you roasted, ground, brewed, and otherwise prepared the artisanal beverage of your choice? (Just water for me, thanks.) Right, let's crack on...

How Do We Run Our Rails App?

Unfortunately, we can't start a Rails server with just the ruby:2.6 image—Rails has a few more requirements. For example, we're going to need a JavaScript interpreter (like Node.js) to help with the asset pipeline, plus we'll need to install our gem dependencies. How do we run a Rails server in a container while making sure that these requirements are satisfied?

There are a few approaches we could take. We *could* do what we did in the previous chapter: run bash inside a container based on the ruby:2.6 image, and install what we need from there. However, running the commands *manually* is not easily repeatable. We want a reliable, repeatable way of spinning up Rails servers left, right, and center. Having to run various manual commands every time we want to start a Rails server just isn't going to cut it.

Another way we *could* get a container to run Rails is by taking that same set of commands needed to install Rails' requirements, and chain them together into a long, compound `docker run` command. However, not only would the command be huge, ugly, and hard to remember, but worst of all, it would be *slow*. The setup instructions would have to be run from scratch every time, including installing Node.js or our gem dependencies. We don't want to have to be waiting minutes just to start a Rails server.

Compound docker run Commands

You may be curious to know how you'd run multiple commands in a container with `docker run`. The problem is that `docker run` is designed to start a container and run a *single* command.

The trick to get around this limitation is to use the `bash` command's `-c` option, which starts a Bash shell and immediately executes whatever you pass in as a string. This lets you do the following:

```
$ docker run <options> [image:version] \
    bash -c "command1 && command2 && command3..."
```

Clever old `bash`.

So what's the *real* solution?

Well, we want to be able to run containers based on a *preconfigured* state that has everything needed in order to run Rails. What we really want is a factory—hint hint—for creating these perfect Rails server containers. Did you get the subtle hint? In the previous chapter, we said that an *image* is a "factory for creating specific containers." Sounds like just what we need.

Defining Our First Custom Image

In real life, a factory doesn't come out of nowhere. It has to be constructed from blueprints: detailed plans and instructions that describe exactly what it's supposed to look like. Docker's container factories—in other words, images—are no different. They require a special blueprint file aptly named a Dockerfile. A Dockerfile uses special syntax to describe exactly how the image should be constructed. If you've heard the expression *infrastructure as code*, this is an example of it: a Dockerfile describes how a machine image is configured as shown in the figure on page 19.

A Dockerfile is made up of various *instructions*—such as FROM, RUN, COPY, and WORKDIR—each capitalized by convention. Rather than talk about them in the abstract, though, let's look at a specific example.

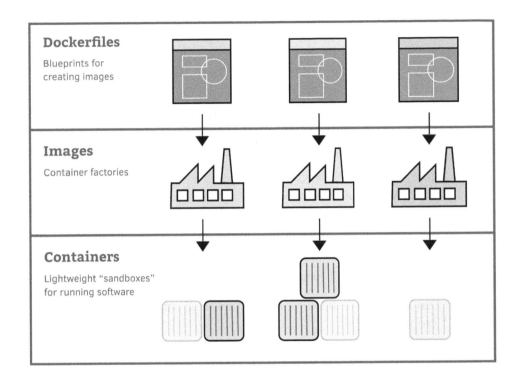

Here's a basic Dockerfile for running our Rails app. It's not perfect—we'll make several improvements in Chapter 3, *Fine-Tuning Our Rails Image*, on page 31—but it's good enough for now. There's no need to create this file; for now we'll just discuss it:

```
FROM ruby:2.6

RUN apt-get update -yqq
RUN apt-get install -yqq --no-install-recommends nodejs

COPY . /usr/src/app/

WORKDIR /usr/src/app
RUN bundle install
```

Every image has to start from something: another, preexisting image. For that reason, every Dockerfile begins with a FROM instruction, which specifies the image to use as its starting point. Typically, we'll look for a starting image that's close to what we need but more general. That way we can extend and customize it to our needs.

The first line of our Dockerfile is

```
FROM ruby:2.6
```

This is saying that our image will be based off the ruby:2.6 image, which, as you've probably guessed, has Ruby 2.6 preinstalled. We've chosen to start from this image because having Ruby installed is our biggest requirement, so this image gets us most of the way there.

Right at the Top: Base Images

There are several special images with no parent image—known as a *base image*—that ultimately all images depend on. They contain the minimal user filesystem for an operating system.

If you want to build your own stripped-down image, you could build your image FROM scratch (reads well, doesn't it?) where scratch is a minimal base image.

It's even possible to create your own base images,[1] although this is an advanced topic. We're not going to cover it since chances are you'll never need to do it.

The next two lines of our Dockerfile are RUN instructions, which tell Docker to execute a command:

```
RUN apt-get update -yqq
RUN apt-get install -yqq --no-install-recommends nodejs
```

Here, we tell Docker to run apt-get update -yqq, followed by apt-get install -yqq --no-install-recommends nodejs—but what do these two commands achieve for us?

As you may already know, apt-get is a command used to install software on Debian (and some other) Linux distributions.[2] We're using it in our Dockerfile because the official Ruby image that our image builds on top of is based on Debian—specifically, a version called Stretch.[3]

The apt-get update command tells the package manager to download the latest package information. Many Dockerfiles will have a similar line, because without it, apt has no package information at all, and therefore won't be able to install anything. The -yqq option is a combination of the -y option, which says to answer "yes" to any prompts, and the -qq option, which enables "quiet" mode to reduce the printed output.

Next, the apt-get install command installs Node.js, a prerequisite for running Rails. The --no-install-recommends says not to install other recommended but

---

1. docs.docker.com/engine/userguide/eng-image/baseimages/

2. https://en.wikipedia.org/wiki/Advanced_Packaging_Tool

3. https://github.com/docker-library/ruby/blob/a04dd5259eaef8d682dae2bb709f03219a6e5905/2.5/stretch/Dockerfile#L1

nonessential packages—we don't need them, and we want to keep our image size as small as possible by not installing unnecessary files.

If you're familiar with apt-get in Linux, you may be wondering why we're not running the commands as root with sudo. That's because, by default, commands inside a container are run by the root user, so sudo is unnecessary (although, as we mention on page 192, this has security implications for production apps).

Let's shift gears briefly before we look at the next line of our Dockerfile.

Remember that images, and the containers they spawn, are separate from our local machine—they are isolated, sandboxed environments. Therefore, we need a way to include some of our local files inside the containers we run.

We've already seen in *Generating a New Rails App Without Ruby Installed*, on page 10, that we can mount a local directory into a running container. A mounted volume acts like a shared directory between the container and the host, and is one way we can make local files accessible inside the container.

However, mounting a volume has a serious downside if it's the only way you get files into a container. Files in a volume aren't part of the image itself; they are overlaid onto the image at *runtime* (when you start a container.) If the mounted files were essential, the image wouldn't function without them, but the whole point of images is to package up everything they need in order to run. Therefore, it's good practice to bake any needed files into the image itself.

The next line in our Dockerfile serves exactly this purpose:

```
COPY . /usr/src/app/
```

This tells Docker to copy all the files from our local, current directory (.) into /usr/src/app on the filesystem of the new image. Since our local, current directory is our Rails root, effectively we're saying, "Copy our Rails app into the container at /usr/src/app." The source path on our local machine is always *relative* to where the Dockerfile is located.

Having added our Rails files into the image at /usr/src/app, we're going to want to run various commands that need to operate in this directory where the files are. For example, soon we'll want to run our app with a Rails server in a container with a command like this:

```
$ docker run [OPTIONS] <our custom image> bin/rails server
```

Unfortunately, this command would fail because, by default, a container's working directory is /, which doesn't contain our Rails app files—we copied those into /usr/src/app.

However, the WORKDIR instruction can help us fix the situation. Effectively, it performs a *change directory* (cd) command, changing what the image considers its current directory. The next line in our Dockerfile uses it to set /usr/src/app as the working directory:

```
WORKDIR /usr/src/app
```

Now running bin/rails server (and similar) commands will work because they will be executed from the correct directory.

You can use multiple WORKDIR instructions in your Dockerfile, each one remaining in effect until another one is issued. The final WORKDIR will be the initial working directory for containers created from the image.

Finally, we come to the last line of our Dockerfile:

```
RUN bundle install
```

The command is executed from the container's current working directory, which in the previous command was set to be /usr/src/app. So this will install the gems defined in our Rails project's Gemfile, which are needed in order to start the application.

Putting It All Together

Armed with all this knowledge, our Dockerfile should now be much more understandable. Let's review it one more time:

```
Line 1 FROM ruby:2.6
     2
     3 RUN apt-get update -yqq
     4 RUN apt-get install -yqq --no-install-recommends nodejs
     5
     6 COPY . /usr/src/app/
     7
     8 WORKDIR /usr/src/app
     9 RUN bundle install
```

First, on line 1, we say that our custom image will use the ruby:2.6 image as its starting point. Next we update the apt package manager's package information (line 3), so it knows where to install things from. Then we use it to install nodejs (line 4), which we need for Rails' asset pipeline.

With the prerequisites for Rails taken care of, we then copy our Rails app files from our local directory into the container at /usr/src/app (line 6) so they are baked into the image. We make this the current working directory for the image (line 8) so that we can execute Rails commands against the image from the correct directory.

Finally, we bundle install (line 9) to install the gems we need for our Rails project.

Now that it makes more sense, let's go ahead and actually create this Dockerfile. First let's make sure we're in the top-level (root) directory of our Rails app:

```
$ ls
Gemfile    Rakefile   bin       config.ru  lib  package.json  storage  vendor
README.md  app        config    db         log  public        tmp
```

Then crack open your editor of choice and create a file called Dockerfile with the contents as shown. I'd highly recommend typing it in by hand rather than copying and pasting—when learning a new skill, physically typing things out helps to cement it in your mind and build up your muscle memory.

With our swanky Dockerfile in hand, let's turn our attention to how we use it to create an actual image.

Building Our Image

The process of generating an image from a Dockerfile is called *building an image*. We do that with the docker build command, which has the following format:

```
$ docker build [options] path/to/build/directory
```

In our case, you should already still be in the directory containing our Dockerfile and project files so we can use a single dot to indicate the current directory. Let's give it a go:

```
$ docker build .
Sending build context to Docker daemon  138.8kB
Step 1/6 : FROM ruby:2.6
 ---> f28a9e1d0449
Step 2/6 : RUN apt-get update -yqq
 ---> Running in 29677ed71d2b
Removing intermediate container 29677ed71d2b
 ---> 761da319d69a
«...»
Step 6/6 : RUN bundle install
 ---> Running in 4550030ac412
«...»
Bundle complete! 15 Gemfile dependencies, 68 gems now installed.
Bundled gems are installed into `/usr/local/bundle`
«...»
Removing intermediate container 4550030ac412
 ---> a1df0eddba18
Successfully built a1df0eddba18
```

Wow, that's quite a lot of output. What is actually happening?

Docker processes our Dockerfile one instruction at a time. The first instruction—FROM—is treated differently from all the others. Docker checks whether we already have the specified image on our local system. If the image isn't available, Docker downloads the image, just like it did in *Running a Ruby Script Without Ruby Installed*, on page 7, when we ran docker run with the ruby:2.6 image for the first time.

All other instructions in the Dockerfile are processed in essentially the same way. Docker starts a throwaway container based on the image created in the previous step, and it executes the current Dockerfile instruction inside it. Then Docker *commits* the changes just made as a result of executing the instruction, creating a new *intermediate image* for this step.

You can see all this happening in the output, which is split into sections: one for each instruction in the Dockerfile. The output for each step follows a very regular format:

```
Line 1  Step <current step>/<total steps> : <Dockerfile instruction>
     2  ---> Running in <container ID>
     3  [Any output from running the instruction]
     4  Removing intermediate container <container ID>
     5  ---> <image ID>
```

For context, we are given the Dockerfile instruction, along with which step this is in the build process (line 1). Next we see the ID of the throwaway container used to execute the current Dockerfile instruction (line 2) followed by any output from running the instruction (line 3).

Every image created—even intermediate ones—are given a unique, randomly generated image ID. This is how Docker identifies images internally, and it gives us a way to refer to them. The ID of the image created in this step is shown on line 5.

Finally, on line 4, Docker tells us that it is deleting the throwaway container it used in this step.

When building a custom image, it's really the final image we're interested in. This represents the final state after all the instructions in the Dockerfile have been executed. That's why the output concludes by giving us the final image ID (if you're following along, your image ID will differ):

```
Successfully built a1df0eddba18
```

That all seems fair enough, but where *is* the image we just built?

The docker build command doesn't output a file; it simply makes the new image available, adding it to the list of images that Docker knows about. Docker manages where and how images are stored on your filesystem. We list the images on our system with the following command:

```
$ docker images
REPOSITORY      TAG        IMAGE ID       CREATED        SIZE
<none>          <none>     a1df0eddba18   1 second ago   1.01GB
ruby            2.6        f28a9e1d0449   6 days ago     868MB
```

The first entry is the custom image that we just built—its image ID matches the one specified at the end of the docker build command.

Running a Rails Server with Our Image

Now that we've created our own tailor-made image, we should be able to start up a Rails server to run our app.

Let's try doing that now.

We can refer to our image by its ID. However, image IDs are long and hard to remember, so normally you would assign a meaningful name to an image. We'll see how to do that later in *Naming and Versioning Our Image*, on page 31. For now, though, referring to our image by its ID is good enough to let us start using the image. Let's crack on and do just that.

Image ID in hand, we can start our Rails app inside a container based on our custom image with the following command. Let's run it now:

```
$ docker run -p 3000:3000 a1df0eddba18 \
    bin/rails s -b 0.0.0.0
```

Aside from the new -p 3000:3000 option, which we'll cover shortly in *Reaching the App: Publishing Ports*, on page 26, this is a plain old docker run command. It says, "Start a container based on our custom image (a1df0eddba18), and run bin/rails s -b 0.0.0.0 inside it." If you haven't seen the -b option before, we'll explain why this is needed in *Binding the Rails Server to IP Addresses*, on page 28.

We should see that Rails starts up correctly:

```
=> Booting Puma
=> Rails 5.2.2 application starting in development
=> Run `rails server -h` for more startup options
Puma starting in single mode...
* Version 3.12.0 (ruby 2.6.0-p0), codename: Llamas in Pajamas
* Min threads: 5, max threads: 5
* Environment: development
* Listening on tcp://0.0.0.0:3000
Use Ctrl-C to stop
```

It does! So far so good.

Now go ahead and visit http://localhost:3000 in your browser. You should see the familiar Rails welcome page.

Yay! You're on Rails!

Rails version: 5.2.2
Ruby version: 2.6.0 (x86_64-linux)

High five! We can reach our app.

In your terminal, you'll see the Rails log output updated to show our request:

```
Started GET "/" for 172.17.0.1 at 2019-01-15 09:49:45 +0000
«...»
  Rendering /usr/local/bundle/gems/railties-5.2.2/lib/rails/templates/rails/
welcome/index.html.erb
  Rendered /usr/local/bundle/gems/railties-5.2.2/lib/rails/templates/rails/
welcome/index.html.erb (2.7ms)
Completed 200 OK in 17ms (Views: 10.0ms | ActiveRecord: 0.0ms)
```

We're in business. You can now stop the Rails server by pressing Ctrl-C.

OK, I've fobbed you off for long enough. It's time to discuss what the various docker run command options we've been using actually do. Got your thinking cap on? Then let's get to it.

Reaching the App: Publishing Ports

As we know, containers are isolated sandboxes. How is it that we're able to reach our app by visiting http://localhost:3000 on our local machine?

The truth is, containers wouldn't be very useful if there was no way of reaching them from outside of Docker. The whole point of a web server, for example, is that it's accessible to people making requests.

Although, by default, a container can only be accessed from within the Docker network it's connected to (more on this in *How Containers Can Talk to Each Other*, on page 63), we can make it accessible externally by *publishing one or more ports* with docker run's -p option.

In our command, we specified -p 3000:3000; this publishes the container's port 3000 (the second number) on port 3000 on our local machine. That means that a request to http://localhost:3000 will reach our Rails server running inside the container on port 3000.

How does this work in practice?

As we saw in the Docker for Linux architecture diagram on page 14, on Linux, the Docker daemon runs directly on the local machine. In this case, publishing a port simply sets up a port mapping (via an iptables rule), which forwards requests to http://localhost:3000 on to the Docker Engine, which knows to route the request to the network the container is on (as shown in the following figure).

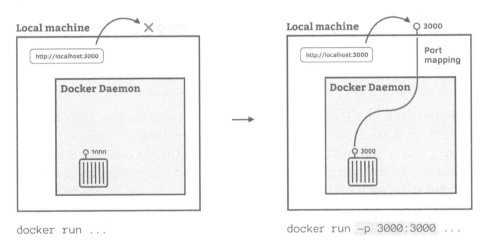

Docker for Mac/Windows has an added complication. Remember, here the Docker daemon is running inside a lightweight Linux VM, as we saw in the Docker for Mac/Windows architecture diagram on page 14. Inside the VM, things work exactly as Docker on Linux—the port mapping will route requests to the container. However, an extra bit of magic is needed to forward requests from http://localhost:3000 to the VM's port 3000; Docker for Mac/Linux sets up port forwarding to achieve this, as illustrated in the figure on page 28.

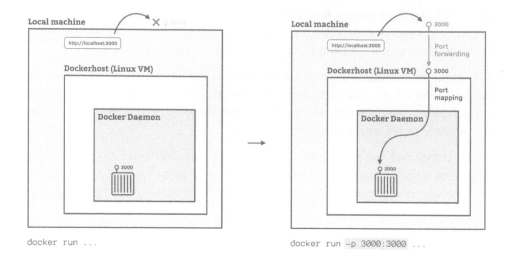

```
docker run ...                          docker run -p 3000:3000 ...
```

When publishing a port, you don't have to use the same external port as the service inside the container. If we had specified -p 80:3000, it would have mapped port 80 on our local machine to the Rails server listening on port 3000 inside the container. This gives us a lot of flexibility in terms of how we expose services to the outside world.

Binding the Rails Server to IP Addresses

Normally, to start a Rails server, we'd simply run bin/rails s, yet when we started the Rails server with docker run, we used bin/rails s -b 0.0.0.0. Why was that?

When you start the Rails server with bin/rails s, by default, it only listens to requests on localhost (or 127.0.0.1) on whatever machine it's running on. This provides a secure default, preventing the Rails app server from being accessible externally. However, in our case, the server is running inside a container, but the request is coming from outside.

When we request http://localhost:3000 on our local machine, as we've just seen in *Reaching the App: Publishing Ports*, on page 26, the request is forwarded to the Docker Engine. This in turn routes the request to the container running the Rails server, by translating the request to [IP address of container]:3000. However, as the Rails server is only listening to requests on localhost, nothing responds to this request coming in for a different IP address.

To fix this, we have to tell our Rails server to *bind* to *all* IP addresses, not just to localhost, using the option -b 0.0.0.0. The IP address 0.0.0.0 is a special address that means *"all IPv4 address on this machine."*

Finding the IP Address of a Running Container

If you're curious how you'd find out the actual IP address of a running container, you can do it as follows:

1. Get the container ID:

```
$ docker ps
CONTAINER ID         IMAGE                «more info»
d7230c4b0595         e28cf982ae39         «.........»
```

2. Use this docker inspect command specifying the container ID:

```
$ docker inspect --format \
    '{{ .NetworkSettings.IPAddress }}' d7230c4b0595
172.17.0.2
```

Quick Recap

Wow, what an action-packed chapter! Let's review the highlights:

1. We saw our first, rough-and-ready Dockerfile designed to allow us to run our app with a Rails server:

```
FROM ruby:2.6

RUN apt-get update -yqq
RUN apt-get install -yqq --no-install-recommends nodejs

COPY . /usr/src/app/

WORKDIR /usr/src/app
RUN bundle install
```

2. We built our custom image from this Dockerfile with:

```
$ docker build .
```

3. We listed the images on our system by issuing:

```
$ docker images
```

4. We started up a Rails server to run our app with:

```
$ docker run -p 3000:3000 a1df0eddba18 \
  bin/rails s -b 0.0.0.0
```

And we saw it running in a browser on http://localhost:3000.

In the next chapter, we'll start to make some further refinements to our Dockerfile. In the process, we'll learn how to give our images friendly names, and speed up image builds by taking advantage of the built-in caching mechanism.

## CHAPTER 3

Fine-Tuning Our Rails Image

We covered a lot of ground in the previous chapter. We saw our first Dockerfile, which we used to build a custom image, tailored for running our Rails app.

However, you may recall that we said this Dockerfile was "good enough" but "not perfect" (*Defining Our First Custom Image*, on page 18). The truth is, we took a few shortcuts for the sake of simplicity. Now that you have some Docker fundamentals under your belt, we can go back and address these issues.

By the end of this chapter, we'll have our Dockerfile looking shipshape and ready for us to dive into the final piece of the development puzzle—Docker Compose—but I'm getting ahead of myself.

So grab some overalls, a trusty wrench, and plenty of spit and polish—you're going to need them, metaphorically speaking that is.

Naming and Versioning Our Image

When we ran our Rails server with this command:

```
$ docker run -p 3000:3000 a1df0eddba18 \
    bin/rails s -b 0.0.0.0
```

we referred to our custom image by its ID: a1df0eddba18 (yours will differ). There's no way we're going to remember that. Just like you wouldn't refer to a Git branch using the SHA-1 hash of its latest commit, the same is true for images. Instead, we give our images human-friendly names by *tagging* them. Let's say we want to name our image railsapp. We can do this by running:

```
$ docker tag a1df0eddba18 railsapp
```

which says, "Tag the image identified by 'a1df0eddba18' with 'railsapp'." To verify this worked, let's list our images with:

```
$ docker images
```

The output confirms that the image name (also known as the *repository*) has been set to railsapp:

```
REPOSITORY      TAG        IMAGE ID       CREATED          SIZE
railsapp        latest     a1df0eddba18   8 minutes ago    1.01GB
«...»
```

Notice that the "tag" field is listed as latest. That's because the docker tag command actually takes as its argument an *image reference*, which is made up of two parts: the image (repo) name, and an optional tag:

```
<image_name>[:<tag>]
```

You can set the tag to any valid string made up of letters, digits, underscores, periods, and dashes (with some caveats).[1] If none is provided, the default tag—latest—will be used.

Unfortunately, the meaning of tag here is slightly overloaded. I recommend thinking of the docker tag command as *tagging* an image with both an image/repository name (in our case, railsapp) *and* a tag (in our case, the default of latest). It's a little bit strange, but you get used to it.

We can give an image as many different tags as we like. For example, let's also give our image the version number 1.0 by running:

```
$ docker tag railsapp railsapp:1.0
```

Here we refer to our image as railsapp since we've already tagged it with that name (railsapp:latest also would have worked). The new tag railsapp:1.0 is made up of the image name railsapp and version 1.0. A quick listing shows this has worked:

```
$ docker images
REPOSITORY      TAG        IMAGE ID       CREATED          SIZE
railsapp        1.0        a1df0eddba18   8 minutes ago    1.01GB
railsapp        latest     a1df0eddba18   8 minutes ago    1.01GB
«...»
```

Although there are two separate lines, showing our railsapp image with both the latest and 1.0 version tags, the "image ID" field confirms that these are one and the same image.

Rather than tagging images after they've been built, we can tag them when we build the image using the -t option. Multiple tags can be specified by adding multiple -t options, so we could have achieved the same result as our two previous docker tag commands if we had built the image with the command:

```
$ docker build -t railsapp -t railsapp:1.0 .
```

---

1. https://docs.docker.com/engine/reference/commandline/tag/#extended-description

Having named our image, we're now able to start our Rails server using the image name, like so:

```
$ docker run -p 3000:3000 railsapp \
    bin/rails s -b 0.0.0.0
```

Ahh. Much better.

Running a specific version of an image is exactly as you'd expect: using the same colon notation as used previously. For example, to explicitly use version 1.0 of our image, we'd run:

```
$ docker run -p 3000:3000 railsapp:1.0 \
    bin/rails s -b 0.0.0.0
```

A Default Command

Currently, every time we want to start a Rails server in a container, we have to explicitly specify the command bin/rails s -b 0.0.0.0 as part of our docker run command:

```
$ docker run -p 3000:3000 railsapp \
    bin/rails s -b 0.0.0.0
```

This is a shame because the *main purpose* of our custom image is to start a Rails server. It would be better if we could embed the knowledge of how to start the Rails server in the image itself.

We can do this by adding a new instruction to our Dockerfile. The CMD instruction, pronounced "command," specifies the *default command* to run when a container is started from the image. Let's use this in our Dockerfile to start the Rails server by default:

```
FROM ruby:2.6

RUN apt-get update -yqq
RUN apt-get install -yqq --no-install-recommends nodejs

COPY . /usr/src/app/

WORKDIR /usr/src/app
RUN bundle install

➤ CMD ["bin/rails", "s", "-b", "0.0.0.0"]
```

Looking at this new line, you may notice the weird array notation used to specify the command. This form—known as the *Exec* form—is needed so that our Rails server is started as the first process in the container (PID 1) and correctly receives Unix signals such as the signal to terminate. It's the recommended form, and most commonly used.

The other form of the CMD instruction, which is rarely used, omits the array notation in favor of writing the command directly:

```
CMD bin/rails s -b 0.0.0.0
```

This is known as the *Shell* form because Docker executes the command via a *command shell*, prefixing it with /bin/sh -c—so in our case, it runs /bin/sh -c bin/rails s -b 0.0.0.0. The problem is that /bin/sh -c, rather than the Rails server, is the first process inside the container; since /bin/sh -c doesn't pass signals on to its subprocesses, this would cause issues when trying to terminate the server. Generally, you can just avoid this form altogether.

OK, let's rebuild our image with our new CMD instruction, remembering to tag as the latest version of railsapp:

```
$ docker build -t railsapp .
Sending build context to Docker daemon  138.8kB
«...»
Successfully built f87ad761cd0f
Successfully tagged railsapp:latest
```

With our newly built image, we can launch the Rails server—omitting the bin/rails s -b 0.0.0.0—with just:

```
$ docker run -p 3000:3000 railsapp
```

It's important to note that the CMD instruction just provides a *default* command—you can specify a different one when you issue the docker run command. For example, to list our Rake tasks, we'd run:

```
$ docker run --rm railsapp bin/rails -T
```

Note the use of --rm to delete the container after it runs. We used it here and not when running the Rails server, because this container has served its purpose after it has generated the Rake task output, whereas a container to run the Rails server can be reused.

Ignoring Unnecessary Files

You may remember that there's a separation between the Docker CLI that we use to run commands, and the Docker daemon that does most of the actual work (as we saw in the architecture diagrams for Docker for Linux on page 14 and Docker for Mac/Windows on page 14). Building an image is no different—it's the Docker daemon that actually builds the image.

How does this work in practice?

When the docker build command is run, the CLI tool takes all the files in the build directory specified—which collectively are known as the *build context*—and sends them to the Docker daemon. The daemon is then able to process the Dockerfile and carry out the instructions in it to generate the image.

We need a way to restrict which files are sent as part of the build context because sending more files slows down your builds (especially true on Docker for Mac or Windows where the daemon is running in a virtualized host). Also, we might want to prevent sensitive files containing secrets from being included in our image—particularly if we plan to share the image publicly.

To exclude certain files and directories from being sent as part of the build context, we list them in a .dockerignore file in our build directory. The .dockerignore file works on a similar basis to a .gitignore file, which you're probably familiar with, although the pattern matching syntax is slightly different.[2]

Let's create a basic .dockerignore file for our project:

```
Line 1   # Git
     -   .git
     -   .gitignore
     -
     5   # Logs
     -   log/*
     -
     -   # Temp files
     -   tmp/*
    10
     -   # Editor temp files
     -   *.swp
     -   *.swo
```

We exclude the .git directory (line 2), which contains the Git history and config, as our image only needs the latest version of the files. Although a minor thing, while we're at it, we've excluded the .gitignore file too (line 3).

Similarly, we exclude any logs (line 6) or temp files (9), as these are generated and can safely be ignored. Finally, I'm excluding Vim's temporary .swp and .swo files (lines 12 and 13)—feel free to do the same for your editor of choice.

This .dockerignore file is a good starting place, but you can really go to town and ignore all cached or generated files.

Let's rebuild our image with the .dockerignore file in place.

---

2. https://docs.docker.com/engine/reference/builder/#dockerignore-file

```
$ docker build -t railsapp .
Sending build context to Docker daemon  102.9kB
《...》
Successfully built 577a1a5a2d2c
Successfully tagged railsapp:latest
```

The size of the build context is reported in the output—102.9 KB—which is smaller than prior to adding the Docker .dockerignore (138.8 KB). The savings will increase over time, especially as the Git history gets larger.

The Image Build Cache

During development, we rebuild our image fairly regularly, either to install new gems (bundle install is one of the steps in our Dockerfile) or to update our dependencies such as Node.js.

Just like a fast test suite helps by reducing the feedback loop, it's important to keep our image builds as fast as possible too. One way that Docker helps is by caching each step in our build, meaning that it only needs to rebuild from the first instruction in the Dockerfile where there is a change. A change could either be literally deleting or modifying the Dockerfile instruction, or it could be associated with filesystem changes, as we'll see shortly.

Since there are no changes to our Dockerfile or files since our last build, it would be extremely fast to rebuild the image now. Each step has already been built and cached, so Docker will have to do very little work.

Let's try rebuilding our image now:

```
$ docker build -t railsapp .
Sending build context to Docker daemon  102.9kB
Step 1/7 : FROM ruby:2.6
 ---> f28a9e1d0449
Step 2/7 : RUN apt-get update -yqq
 ---> Using cache
 ---> 761da319d69a
Step 3/7 : RUN apt-get install -yqq --no-install-recommends nodejs
 ---> Using cache
 ---> 145b025f550c
Step 4/7 : COPY . /usr/src/app/
 ---> Using cache
 ---> 045a92afdc82
Step 5/7 : WORKDIR /usr/src/app
 ---> Using cache
 ---> 1d89cb7f0720
Step 6/7 : RUN bundle install
 ---> Using cache
 ---> 81ad2d531548
```

```
Step 7/7 : CMD ["bin/rails", "s", "-b", "0.0.0.0"]
 ---> Using cache
 ---> 577a1a5a2d2c
Successfully built 577a1a5a2d2c
Successfully tagged railsapp:latest
```

The image should build very quickly. If you look at the output, you'll see that for each step (other than the FROM instruction), it explicitly says Using cache. This indicates that Docker didn't need to create a new image for that step; it simply reused an intermediate image cached from a previous build.

The cache for a given step is invalidated when you modify the Dockerfile instruction to something that hasn't been built before. Additionally, COPY instructions can have their cache invalidated if copied files have changed since the step was last built. The comparison is made by the Docker daemon based on files in the build context—so ignoring irrelevant files in your .dockerignore file can also prevent cache invalidations.

Since a Dockerfile is sequential, with each instruction building on the previous (intermediate) image, when the cache is invalidated for one step, Docker must rebuild *every subsequent step*. It therefore hurts more when an earlier step is invalidated, because Docker has more steps to rebuild.

Understanding this is useful for keeping our image builds fast as we develop, without taking unnecessary *hits* from busting the image build cache.

In fact, our Dockerfile already has a slight issue with how the caching works…

Caching Issue 1: Updating Packages

Currently, our Dockerfile has the following two lines:

```
RUN apt-get update -yqq
RUN apt-get install -yqq --no-install-recommends nodejs
```

Although this works, there's a hidden problem lurking. Let's say we come along at a later stage and realize we need to install an extra package—for example, the Vim editor. We add the vim package to the apt-get install RUN instruction, busting the cache and causing that instruction to be rerun:

```
RUN apt-get update -yqq
RUN apt-get install -yqq --no-install-recommends nodejs vim
```

However, the apt-get update RUN instruction remains unchanged, and the cached repository details will be used. Rather than getting the current, latest version of the new package we've added, we'll be getting whatever was the latest *at the time we last built our image*. That behavior is almost never what we want.

For that reason, it's recommended to always combine the apt-get update and apt-get install commands into a single RUN instruction like so:[3]

```
RUN apt-get update -yqq && \
  apt-get install -yqq --no-install-recommends nodejs vim
```

This ensures that whenever you change the packages being installed, you'll also get the latest repository information at the same time.

Finally, it's good practice to format the apt-get install command as follows:

```
RUN apt-get update -yqq && apt-get install -yqq --no-install-recommends \
  nodejs \
  vim
```

Using one package per line and keeping packages in alphabetical order makes it easier to see which packages are installed, and locate ones that need to be changed if you have many packages installed.

Let's fix this issue in our Dockerfile now. We don't actually need Vim installed currently, so our two RUN instructions for apt-get update and apt-get install will become:

```
RUN apt-get update -yqq && apt-get install -yqq --no-install-recommends \
  nodejs
```

Let's rebuild our image to include this change:

```
$ docker build -t railsapp .
Sending build context to Docker daemon  102.9kB
Step 1/6 : FROM ruby:2.6
 ---> f28a9e1d0449
«...»
Successfully built 621ceaca3298
Successfully tagged railsapp:latest
```

Caching Issue 2: Unnecessary Gem Installs

Imagine that we want to make a change to our README.md file. Open this file in an editor, and replace the Rails default version with the following:

```
# README

This is a sample Rails application from Docker for Rails Developers (PragProg).
It was generated using Docker without Ruby installed on the local machine.

We're using the app to discover the wonderful world of Rails with Docker.
```

Now let's try something. What happens if we rebuild our image:

---

3. https://docs.docker.com/develop/develop-images/dockerfile_best-practices/#run

```
$ docker build -t railsapp .
Sending build context to Docker daemon  102.9kB
Step 1/6 : FROM ruby:2.6
 ---> f28a9e1d0449
Step 2/6 : RUN apt-get update -yqq && apt-get install -yqq --no-install-
recommends   nodejs
 ---> Using cache
 ---> 29c3dee2b8c7
Step 3/6 : COPY . /usr/src/app/
 ---> fff98079f6ac
Step 4/6 : WORKDIR /usr/src/app
 ---> Running in 3e36b19fecbf
Removing intermediate container 3e36b19fecbf
 ---> 34e46dae43ab
Step 5/6 : RUN bundle install
 ---> Running in f4528be7eb2b
«...»
Bundle complete! 15 Gemfile dependencies, 68 gems now installed.
Bundled gems are installed into `/usr/local/bundle`
«...»
Removing intermediate container f4528be7eb2b
 ---> 5965a3004093
Step 6/6 : CMD ["bin/rails", "s", "-b", "0.0.0.0"]
 ---> Running in fe59ed9392a7
Removing intermediate container fe59ed9392a7
 ---> 1fbb2af53579
Successfully built 1fbb2af53579
Successfully tagged railsapp:latest
```

Wow, that took quite a while. The biggest cause of this slowness was that all our gems were rebuilt from scratch, yet all we did was change our README.md file—what gives?

If you look through the output, you'll see that steps 1 to 3 all say Using cache. Docker didn't have to rebuild those layers because it could compare the Dockerfile instruction with the cached intermediate image for that step, and see that they were the same.

However, that's not the case with step 4 (COPY . /usr/src/app)—this step isn't using the cache. Although the Dockerfile instruction remained the same, since it's a COPY instruction, Docker checks the files being copied (excluding any in the .dockerignore file) and compares them with those copied previously. It realizes that README.md has changed, so it knows to rebuild from this step.

There's no getting around the fact that, if files change, a new image needs to be created containing the changed files. However, in our case, it's unfortunate that merely changing the README.md causes bundle install to be run again. It's both slow and completely unnecessary: our change to README.md had no impact on the gem dependencies. The only reason it's being rerun is because an earlier step was invalidated in our Dockerfile.

Let's see if there's something we can do about this problem.

The Gemfile Caching Trick

It turns out there's an effective way to prevent changes to unrelated files busting our cache and causing a rebuild of all our gems from scratch. The trick is to *separate the copying of files that should* trigger a rebuild of our gems from those that *shouldn't*.

Let's update our Dockerfile to do this:

```
Line 1  FROM ruby:2.6

        RUN apt-get update -yqq && apt-get install -yqq --no-install-recommends \
          nodejs
     5
        COPY Gemfile* /usr/src/app/
        WORKDIR /usr/src/app
        RUN bundle install

    10  COPY . /usr/src/app/

        CMD ["bin/rails", "s", "-b", "0.0.0.0"]
```

The first three instructions remain the same, but line 6 is new. It copies our Gemfile and Gemfile.lock into our image *before* the rest of our code.

```
COPY Gemfile* /usr/src/app/
```

This creates a separate, independent layer. Docker's cache for this layer will only be busted if either of these two files change.

Having copied our Gemfile and Gemfile.lock into our image, we can now change into the directory where they are and install our gems:

```
WORKDIR /usr/src/app
RUN bundle install
```

Finally, with our gems installed, we can copy the remainder of our source files into the image:

```
COPY . /usr/src/app/
```

Now, changes to all remaining files copied in this step will only bust the cache at *this* instruction, which is *after* our gems have been installed—just what we want.

Now, let's rebuild our image using this updated Dockerfile. Remember, though, that we've now changed all except the first three instructions in the Dockerfile, so we're expecting the cache to be busted after that. This means that the remaining steps will have to be built from scratch, including the bundle install, which will take some time.

```
$ docker build -t railsapp .
```

With our newly built image, let's see what happens when we modify our README.md file again. Go ahead and make any minor change to README.md, save the change, and then rebuild the image:

```
$ docker build -t railsapp .
Sending build context to Docker daemon  102.9kB
Step 1/7 : FROM ruby:2.6
 ---> f28a9e1d0449
Step 2/7 : RUN apt-get update -yqq && apt-get install -yqq --no-install-
recommends   nodejs
 ---> Using cache
 ---> 29c3dee2b8c7
Step 3/7 : COPY Gemfile* /usr/src/app/
 ---> Using cache
 ---> 050a87002be1
Step 4/7 : WORKDIR /usr/src/app
 ---> Using cache
 ---> d227daeedb1e
Step 5/7 : RUN bundle install
 ---> Using cache
 ---> 616b88058c4b
Step 6/7 : COPY . /usr/src/app/
 ---> b189758b9ded
Step 7/7 : CMD ["bin/rails", "s", "-b", "0.0.0.0"]
 ---> Running in fad4be04ab20
Removing intermediate container fad4be04ab20
 ---> 9be0cf184e64
Successfully built 9be0cf184e64
Successfully tagged railsapp:latest
```

That was much faster than when we changed the README.md earlier. This time, it didn't result in the gems being rebuilt. Lines 6–8 in the Dockerfile could use the cache because nothing had changed at that point. Docker just has to rebuild the final two steps, both of which are fast.

The Finishing Touch

Our Dockerfile is glorious, isn't it? A masterpiece. This little baby is going to get our Rails app development really going places. So let's do what all true artists do and sign our work.

Unlike a painter who signs the bottom right of their canvas, Docker aficionados typically assert their authorship of an image by setting a *maintainer label* as the second instruction. A label is simply a piece of metadata associated with an image.

We set a label using the LABEL instruction, which has the following format:

```
LABEL <key>=<value>
```

This gives the image a label named key set to value.

To indicate who is responsible for maintaining the file, we would modify our Dockerfile to specify their email address like so (you can substitute your email address instead of mine):

```
FROM ruby:2.6
➤ LABEL maintainer="rob@DockerForRailsDevelopers.com"
RUN apt-get update -yqq && apt-get install -yqq --no-install-recommends \
  nodejs
COPY Gemfile* /usr/src/app/
WORKDIR /usr/src/app
RUN bundle install

COPY . /usr/src/app/

CMD ["bin/rails", "s", "-b", "0.0.0.0"]
```

And with that, our Dockerfile is complete.

It's worth noting that labels can be used to store any kind of metadata you like on your images. You can use as many LABEL instructions as you like, or combine them into a single line like so:

```
LABEL <key>=<value> <key>=<value> <key>=<value> ...
```

The choice is yours.

Before we finish up, remember to rebuild your image with this change:

```
$ docker build -t railsapp .
```

On this occasion, because we're introducing a new instruction early in our Dockerfile, the build will necessarily be slower as the gems do have to be installed from scratch.

Quick Recap

Our Dockerfile scrubs up pretty well. You can put the wrench down, take off those oil-stained overalls, and put your feet up—again, metaphorically speaking. You deserve it.

Let's review what we covered:

1. We saw how to name and version our images by giving them tags, either after they're built:

   ```
   $ docker tag a1df0eddba18 railsapp
   ```

   or at build time (here setting two tags):

   ```
   $ docker build -t railsapp -t railsapp:1.0 .
   ```

2. We added a default command to our image using the CMD instruction:

   ```
   CMD ["bin/rails", "s", "-b", "0.0.0.0"]
   ```

3. We sped up our image builds by using a .dockerignore to prevent unnecessary files from being sent to the Docker daemon as part of our build context.

4. We ensured that we always use up-to-date package repository information when altering the packages we install by combining apt-get update and apt-get install into a single RUN instruction:

   ```
   RUN apt-get update -yqq && apt-get install -yqq --no-install-recommends \
       nodejs
   ```

5. We prevented file changes from causing our gems to be rebuilt by copying our Gemfiles earlier in our Dockerfile so they could be cached separately:

   ```
   COPY Gemfile* /usr/src/app/
   WORKDIR /usr/src/app
   RUN bundle install
   ```

6. Finally, we indicated who was responsible for our image by setting a maintainer with the LABEL instruction:

   ```
   LABEL maintainer="rob@DockerForRailsDevelopers.com"
   ```

Not bad for a day's work.

If you thought using Docker for development couldn't get any better, or perhaps still have some reservations, brace yourselves. Up next, we'll discover an even more powerful tool that will supercharge our development. Onward!

## CHAPTER 4

Describing Our App Declaratively with Docker Compose

We've seen how to start containers using the docker run command. However, this is limited to starting a single container at a time. While that's great for one-off tasks, as developers, our applications are typically made up of multiple components, or in Docker terminology, *services*. For example, in addition to our Rails server, we typically need at least a database.

Once you're thinking about an application as a whole, running containers with docker run becomes too cumbersome. We need a different, higher-level tool that lets us coordinate and manage containers for the different services that make up our application.

Enter Docker Compose.

Getting Started with Compose

Docker Compose—or just Compose for short—is a tool for managing an application that needs several different containers to work together. Compose is declarative: you describe each part of your application—known as a *service*—and Compose handles the grunt work of ensuring the right containers are run when and how you need. It also manages creating and destroying the resources needed for the app. For example, it creates a separate, private network for your application, giving you a predictable, isolated environment. As we'll see in Part II, *Toward Production*, on page 127, it also plays a key role in how we deploy and scale applications with Docker.

Compose is designed with developers in mind. It lets us interact with our application in terms of concepts we're familiar with—for example, "run our web service" or "stop the database." This is in stark contrast to the low-level docker run commands we've seen, where the context of what we're trying to achieve is harder to see.

Before we can get Compose to do our bidding, though, we first have to describe our application by creating a docker-compose.yml file. This doesn't replace the need for Dockerfiles—blueprints for creating containers—but it describes what images our app requires and how they are run in concert.

Here's an initial docker-compose.yml for our Rails project:

```
Line 1  version: '3'
     2
     3  services:
     4
     5    web:
     6      build: .
     7      ports:
     8        - "3000:3000"
```

A Compose file always starts with a version number (line 1), which specifies the file format being used. This helps ensure that apps continue to run as expected as new features, or breaking changes, are added to Compose. We're using version 3—the latest major version at the time of writing.[1]

Next we have a collection called services (line 3), which is used to group the constituent parts of our application. Currently, our Rails app *is* our entire app, so we're declaring a single service—which we've chosen to call web—to represent it (line 5). We'll soon be adding another service in Chapter 5, *Beyond the App: Adding Redis*, on page 59.

Nested under web are its various configuration options (lines 6–8).

The first of these:

```
build: .
```

tells Compose where to find the Dockerfile it should use to build our image. The path we specify is relative to the docker-compose.yml file. In this case, it's in the same directory.

Next we come to lines 7–8:

```
ports:
  - "3000:3000"
```

---

1. https://docs.docker.com/compose/compose-file/compose-versioning/

This is equivalent to the -p 3000:3000 option we specified in our docker run command. If you recall, this was used to map the container's port 3000 to port 3000 on our local machine. It's needed to make our Rails app accessible from our local machine.

Launching Our App

With our docker-compose.yml in hand, Compose is now set up to manage our application. However, before we start our app, first a tiny bit of housekeeping. By default, Ruby buffers output to stdout, which doesn't play well with Compose.[2] Let's fix this by switching off Ruby's output buffering.

Add the following line to the top of your config/boot.rb file:

```
$stdout.sync = true
```

With that out of the way, we're ready to launch our app. Instead of the long docker run command, we can now use:

```
$ docker-compose up
```

Before we go through the output, let's discuss what this command does.

When you run docker-compose up, Compose makes sure that the necessary resources have been set up, creating any that are missing before launching a container for each service.

Specifically, it:

1. Creates a separate network just for the app

2. Creates any non-locally mounted volumes defined for the app (we don't have any yet—more on this in Chapter 6, *Adding a Database: Postgres*, on page 71)

3. Builds an image for any services with a build directive

4. Creates a container for each service

5. Launches a container per service

Pretty impressive for a single command.

If we turn our attention back to the output of the command, we can see much of this happening. First the network is created:

```
Creating network "myapp_default" with the default driver
```

---

2. https://github.com/sinatra/sinatra/issues/1118

By convention, Compose names the network <appname>_default, where appname is inferred from the containing directory.

Next it builds the image for our web service:

```
Building web
Step 1/8 : FROM ruby:2.6
 ---> f28a9e1d0449
Step 2/8 : LABEL maintainer="rob@DockerForRailsDevelopers.com"
 ---> Using cache
 ---> d69ea7d90f89
Step 3/8 : RUN apt-get update -yqq && apt-get install -yqq --no-install-
recommends   nodejs
 ---> Using cache
 ---> 463750079bef
«...»
Step 8/8 : CMD ["bin/rails", "s", "-b", "0.0.0.0"]
 ---> Running in b11e989011fc
Removing intermediate container b11e989011fc
 ---> a18b3079c84b
Successfully built a18b3079c84b
```

Compose gives the image a name and version by tagging it:

```
Successfully tagged myapp_web:latest
```

using the convention <appname>_<service_name>:latest, again inferring the appname from the enclosing directory. In our case, this becomes myapp_web:latest.

You can verify that the myapp_web image was created by running the following in a separate terminal window:

```
$ docker images
```

You should see it listed in one of the lines of the output:

```
REPOSITORY      TAG        IMAGE ID        CREATED            SIZE
myapp_web       latest     a18b3079c84b    About a minute ago  1.01GB
...
```

Compose will only build images if they don't exist, which will either be because it's the first time you've run docker-compose up or because you've deleted them. This is an important point: you are responsible for rebuilding your images as needed (see *Rebuilding Our Images*, on page 55); in fact, Compose reminds us of this in the output:

```
WARNING: Image for service web was built because it did not already exist.
To rebuild this image you must use `docker-compose build` or `docker-compose
up --build`.
```

Next, Compose creates and starts a single container for our web service based on the image it has just created. It will name containers using the format <appname>_<service name>_<n>:

```
Creating myapp_web_1 ... done
```

In a process known as *attaching*, Compose then connects our local IO streams (stdin, stdout, and stderr) to the running container, so we can see its output:

```
Attaching to myapp_web_1
```

As a result, we're able to see our Rails server starting inside the container:

```
web_1  | => Booting Puma
web_1  | => Rails 5.2.2 application starting in development
web_1  | => Run `rails server -h` for more startup options
web_1  | Puma starting in single mode...
web_1  | * Version 3.12.0 (ruby 2.6.0-p0), codename: Llamas in Pajamas
web_1  | * Min threads: 5, max threads: 5
web_1  | * Environment: development
web_1  | * Listening on tcp://0.0.0.0:3000
web_1  | Use Ctrl-C to stop
```

The Rails server launched thanks to the default CMD instruction we set up in *A Default Command*, on page 33. We could have specified the command directly in the docker-compose.yml file by setting a command option for web—this would have overridden the CMD instruction specified in the Dockerfile.

Go ahead and verify that our app is running: visit http://localhost:3000 in the browser. You should see the familiar Rails welcome page again.

Great! Our docker-compose.yml is working and everything is hunky-dory.

You can then terminate Compose by pressing Ctrl-C; you should see the containers being shut down.

Containers Not Shutting Down Gracefully

Unfortunately, Compose has an intermittent issue you'll need to watch out for. Occasionally, on terminating Compose with Ctrl-C, you may see ^CERROR: Aborting and find the containers aren't shut down. Unfortunately, if this happens, you'll have to stop the containers manually with docker-compose stop. See Chapter 9 for more details.

There's no need to run this now, but if we don't care about viewing the container output, we can start the containers in *detached* mode by specifying the -d option. This launches the application in the background and returns you to the shell prompt.

```
$ docker-compose up -d
Starting myapp_web_46768de21d89 ... done
```

Note, however, that it may take some time for Rails to launch and the application to become available.

Problem Starting Rails?

 If you encounter an error on starting the server that says something like, "A server is already running," you've run into a bug with Compose. For now, simply delete the tmp/pids/server.pid on your local machine. See Chapter 9 for a better solution.

Mounting a Local Volume

Before we leave our docker-compose.yml, let's make a small addition.

We've already seen how to mount a local directory inside a container with docker run by using the -v option—we did this in *Generating a New Rails App Without Ruby Installed*, on page 10, so that the Rails project files generated inside the container would be available on our local machine.

A mounted local volume represents some filesystem that's shared between your local machine and the container. Files in the mounted volume are synced both ways between your local filesystem and the container. Because of this, a local volume mount can allow us to develop locally and have the Rails server running in the container automatically pick up the file changes without restarting—just like we're used to.

We are going to set up this locally mounted volume using Compose rather than using docker run this time. In our docker run command, we used the option -v $PWD:/usr/src/app to mount our current, local directory inside the Rails container at /usr/src/app. We can achieve the same with Compose by adding the following to our docker-compose.yml:

```
version: '3'

services:

  web:
    build: .
    ports:
      - "3000:3000"
    volumes:
      - .:/usr/src/app
```

Here we specify our volume mapping under the volumes property we've added for the web service. Although the volume mapping is very similar to the docker run option we used, there is one slight difference. We were able to refer to the current directory by simply using a period (.) instead of the $PWD environment variable. Compose allows for relative paths like this based on where the docker-compose.yml is located—a nice little bonus.

On relaunching our app with this change:

```
$ docker-compose up -d
```

we're now able to follow the typical development flow of editing files locally and immediately seeing the changes simply by reloading the browser.

Rails Server Not Starting?

 On starting Rails, it's possible you may encounter the same issue mentioned earlier. If Rails thinks the server is already running, you'll need to delete tmp/pids/server.pid on your local machine. We'll see a better way to handle this in Chapter 9.

Starting and Stopping Services

A common thing we'll need to do while developing our application is to stop or start the various services that make it up. In a moment, we'll dive into the fine-grained control Compose gives us to do this. Before we do, though, it's helpful to have in mind the journey that containers go through, from creation until they are no longer needed.

The following figure shows a simplified version of a container's life cycle:

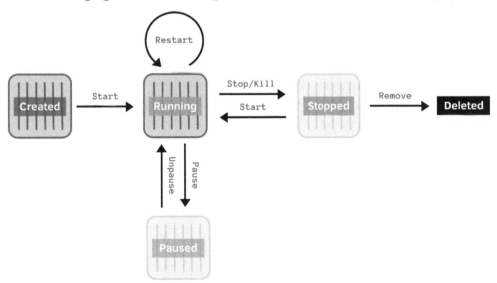

A container comes into existence in the *created* state. It doesn't execute any code; it merely sits around waiting until it's called for. When the container is started, it moves into the *running* state, where it actively executes code. The docker run command we've seen creates a new container, then starts it running.

In the running state, a container can be restarted, stopped, killed, or paused. Pausing a container suspends the running processes so that they can be resumed some time later. Stopping a container attempts to shut down gracefully by sending a terminate signal (SIGTERM) to the main process inside the container—falling back to a forceful shutdown with a kill signal (SIGKILL) if this fails. Killing a container jumps straight to the forceful termination.

A container moves into the *stopped* state if it is stopped, or killed, or if the main process running inside it terminates. The stopped state is similar to the created state: the container sits there doing nothing until it is called upon. From there, the container can either be restarted or, if you have no more use for it, removed from the system. With that in mind, let's see how this works in practice using Compose.

First of all, let's check what containers are currently running. To do this, we use the ps command:

```
$ docker-compose ps
    Name              Command          State          Ports
-------------------------------------------------------------------
myapp_web_1    bin/rails s -b 0.0.0.0    Up      0.0.0.0:3000->3000/tcp
```

The listing includes the container name, the command used to start it, its current state, and its port mappings. Here you can see the container for our Rails server; it's still running from when we previously ran docker-compose up -d (Up means it's running).

If we now wanted to stop the Rails server, we'd do so with the stop command. By default, the command would apply to *all* services listed in our docker-compose.yml file. For example, to stop all containers in the entire application, we would run:

```
$ docker-compose stop
```

To target a *particular* service, we'd specify the service name after the action like so:

```
$ docker-compose stop <service_name>
```

This may seem like a moot point since, currently, web is the only service we have defined. However, we'll soon be adding more services, starting in Chapter 5, *Beyond the App: Adding Redis*, on page 59. It's common to want to target commands at a specific service, so it's very useful to remember this pattern—particularly as all the docker-compose commands follow it.

Let's go ahead and stop the web service:

```
$ docker-compose stop web
Stopping myapp_web_1 ... done
```

Loading localhost:3000 in the browser will now fail, and listing the containers will report that the Rails server has terminated:

```
$ docker-compose ps
    Name              Command          State    Ports
-----------------------------------------------------------
myapp_web_1   bin/rails s -b 0.0.0.0   Exit 1
```

Having stopped a container, we can start it again with the start command:

```
$ docker-compose start web
Starting web ... done
```

There's also a restart command that's handy if, for example, you've made some config changes and want the Rails server to pick them up.

```
$ docker-compose restart web
Restarting myapp_web_1 ... done
```

The various Compose commands we've seen all rely on underlying docker commands.[3] However, we won't cover those in detail since we'll be using Compose from now on. Compose gives us all the power of the lower-level docker commands, but with simpler, app-centric commands.

Other Common Tasks

Besides starting and stopping our services, there are a few more things that we do frequently as part of our day-to-day development. We're going to take a whistle-stop tour of the highlights, since we'll be needing them in the upcoming chapters.

Viewing the Container Logs

We've seen that the docker-compose up, without the -d option, attaches to the containers it starts and follows their output. However, there's also a dedicated command for viewing the container output, which is more flexible.

Let's view the container logs:

```
$ docker-compose logs -f web
```

---

3. https://docs.docker.com/engine/reference/commandline/start/

You should see some output showing the Rails server starting up, similar to:

```
web_1  | => Booting Puma
web_1  | => Rails 5.2.2 application starting in development
web_1  | => Run `rails server -h` for more startup options
web_1  | Puma starting in single mode...
web_1  | * Version 3.12.0 (ruby 2.6.0-p0), codename: Llamas in Pajamas
web_1  | * Min threads: 5, max threads: 5
web_1  | * Environment: development
web_1  | * Listening on tcp://0.0.0.0:3000
web_1  | Use Ctrl-C to stop
```

The -f flag tells the command to follow the output—that is, to stay connected and continue to append to the screen any new output to the logs, similar to the tail Unix command.

Press Ctrl-C to terminate the logging stream.

It's important to realize this command displays the *container output* logs rather than the Rails server logs, which, by default, are stored in the log/ directory. However, as we'll see later, in Part II, *Toward Production*, on page 127, it's common to configure Rails to log to stdout when using Docker.

Check out Docker's documentation[4] for more docker logs options.

Running One-Off Commands

Up until now, we've only run our web container using the image's default CMD, which starts a Rails server. What if we need to run a different command? For example, frequently we'll want to do things like migrate our database with db:migrate, run our tests, update our gems, or perform the many Rails commands we're used to running as part of our development. How do we do that?

There are actually two different ways to achieve this, which we'll demonstrate with a trivial example: echoing something to the screen. Don't let this trivial example fool you; the approaches use the same mechanism we'll employ to run all our favorite commands in the upcoming chapters.

First, we can use docker run to start a new container for our one-off command. We provide the command after the service name, as follows, which overrides any default commands specified either in the docker-compose.yml file or in the Dockerfile itself:

```
$ docker-compose run --rm web echo 'ran a different command'
ran a different command
```

---

4.   https://docs.docker.com/engine/reference/commandline/logs/

The echo command executed successfully. Notice that, unlike when we're running the Rails server, the container terminates immediately after running the command. That's because the echo command completes and returns its exit status, whereas the Rails server's run loop keeps it executing until you ask it to stop (or it crashes). Additionally, since this is a one-off command, we've used the --rm option to delete the container once it completes—otherwise, we'll end up with lots of extra containers lying about.

The second way to run a one-off command avoids starting up a new container altogether. Instead, it relies on a running container, and executes the command on that. This is done with the docker-compose exec command.

Assuming our Rails server is running, we can run our echo example like this:

```
$ docker-compose exec web echo 'ran a different command'
ran a different command
```

Although this only works if a container is already running, since it doesn't start a new container, we don't have to remember to clean up additional containers or use the --rm option.

Rebuilding Our Images

We can ask Compose to build our images for us instead of using the underlying docker build command. This is useful to avoid switching between docker and docker-compose commands, but also because our app may contain Dockerfiles for more than one service; our docker-compose.yml file will keep track of which Dockerfile is used for which service.

To rebuild our Rails app server image, known to Compose as our web service, you would issue the command:

```
$ docker-compose build web
```

There are a few different reasons why you may need to rebuild your image. Often, it's because you've updated your Gemfile and need to reinstall your gems (the Dockerfile contains the bundle install command). Occasionally, it's because you have to modify your Dockerfile to install additional dependencies. Or sometimes you want to share your image and need to include the latest code changes (thanks to the Dockerfile COPY instruction), as we'll see in Part II, *Toward Production*, on page 127.

Cleaning Up After Ourselves

You may recall that when we first issue the docker-compose up for a project, it creates a network, the volumes, and any containers needed for the app. The corresponding docker-compose down command stops any running containers and removes them along with the app's dedicated network and volumes.

This is useful when you're done with a project and want to free up space that its resources were using. If you just want to remove the app's containers, there's the docker-compose rm command for this purpose.

Pruning: Freeing Up Unused Resources

Since we're talking about freeing up resources, there are some other commands that help us with this aim.

As we change our Dockerfile and rebuild images, some images inevitably will no longer be needed or used, yet sit there taking up precious disk space. These are known as *dangling* images; they can be removed with the docker image prune[5] command.

There's an entire family of prune commands to free up other unused resources (for example, docker container prune).[6] There's even a single command to free up all resources in one go:[7]

```
$ docker system prune
```

Quick Recap

We've introduced a powerful new tool into our arsenal: Docker Compose. It really is a one-stop-shop command for developing our app with Docker.

Let's review what we covered. In this chapter:

1. We introduced the docker-compose.yml and its format.

2. We created our own docker-compose.yml for our Rails app, including a locally mounted volume to allow live editing of local files.

3. We saw how to spin up our entire app and start the Rails server by using the command:

    ```
    $ docker-compose up
    ```

4. We learned various commands for managing our app with Compose:

    *   List running containers

        ```
        $ docker-compose ps
        ```

---

5.   https://docs.docker.com/engine/reference/commandline/image_prune/

6.   https://docs.docker.com/engine/reference/commandline/container_prune/

7.   https://docs.docker.com/engine/reference/commandline/system_prune/

- Manage container life cycle

  ```
  $ docker-compose [start|stop|kill|restart|pause|unpause|rm] \
                  <service name>
  ```

- View the logs

  ```
  $ docker-compose logs [-f] <service name>
  ```

- Run a one-off command in a *new, throwaway container*

  ```
  $ docker-compose run --rm <service name> <some command>
  ```

- Run a one-off command in an *existing container*

  ```
  $ docker-compose exec <service name> <some command>
  ```

- Rebuild an image

  ```
  $ docker-compose build <service name>
  ```

By making use of this Compose goodness, we've replaced our more complicated docker run commands with something clean, easy to remember, and manageable. We can now launch our entire app from scratch with just a single command:

```
$ docker-compose up
```

Hurrah!

Now it's time to start using Compose to extend the capabilities of our app by adding services.

CHAPTER 5

Beyond the App: Adding Redis

OK, fess up. Did you look at the title of this chapter and think "Redis?! What about setting up the database?!" If so, I promise I'm not crazy: there's a very good reason for tackling Redis first, as you'll discover shortly.

First, let's review what we've achieved. We've already learned how to:

- Use Docker to generate a fresh Rails project without Ruby installed
- Start the Ruby server to run our application
- Ensure our gems are installed and up to date
- Create our very own Docker image suited to running our Rails app
- Use Docker Compose to manage the whole process

That's not a bad start, but currently it isn't enough to build anything other than the most basic of websites or apps. We're missing a key piece of the puzzle: how to connect our Rails app to external services like...a database. In this chapter, you'll learn how to do just that, starting with Redis (if you're not familiar with Redis, it's an in-memory, key-value store commonly used for pub/sub messaging, queues, caching, and more—all the cool kids use it, and after this chapter, you will too).

Why Redis before a database? Because, while the process of adding services to our app is similar, it turns out that Redis is *easier to integrate* into our app than a database. Take my word for it: doing it this way around will give you a smoother ride.

In fact, this chapter teaches the basic skills to add *any* service to your app, be it a database (which we'll do in the very next chapter), background workers, Elasticsearch, or even a separate JavaScript front end. Soon our Docker-fueled apps will be every bit as powerful as we're used to, and then some.

Props to Aanand

 The demo app used in this chapter was inspired by Aanand Prasad's demo, which shows how to connect a basic Python Flask app to Redis using Compose.[1]

Aanand is the creator of *Fig*—the precursor to Docker Compose— and a former employee of Docker.

Starting a Redis Server

So we want our Rails app to talk to Redis, huh? Well, first we're going to need a Redis server that our application can talk to. As you might expect, we're not going to install and run Redis on our local machine. Instead, let's leverage the power of Docker and start a Redis server inside a container.

Ultimately, we want to add Redis as a new service with Compose. However, since this is the first we've added, we're going to take baby steps. We'll start by seeing how to run Redis in a container using docker run before we circle back to get Compose to do this for us automatically. As you gain more experience and confidence, you'll be able to skip this first step and jump straight to setting up a service in Compose.

Using docker run

To start a Redis server with docker run, we'd issue the following command:

```
$ docker run --name redis-container redis
```

This command should mostly be familiar: it tells Docker to run a container based on the official Docker redis image.[2] However, there are a couple of options we haven't seen before.

Docker gives each new container a unique *container ID* to identify it. However, these long identifiers aren't very human-friendly. Just like when we tagged an image to give it a friendlier name on page 31, the --name option tells Docker to give our new container a nice, human-readable name.

Now stop the Redis server by pressing Ctrl-C.

Our ultimate aim is for our docker-compose.yml file to fully describe our application, including all its dependencies. Having seen how to start a Redis server with docker run, we're ready to set up Compose to manage Redis for us.

---

1. www.slideshare.net/Docker/compose-breakout-aanand-prasad#8
2. https://hub.docker.com/_/redis/

Let's review our docker-compose.yml file:

```
version: '3'
services:
  web:
    build: .
    ports:
      - "3000:3000"
    volumes:
      - .:/usr/src/app
```

Let's modify it to include a new service that we'll call redis:

```
version: '3'
services:
  web:
    build: .
    ports:
      - "3000:3000"
    volumes:
      - .:/usr/src/app
➤   redis:
➤     image: redis
```

The definition for our new redis service is quite different from that of our web service. For a start, it's a lot simpler; it only has a single property called image.

When defining a service, there are two ways to specify the image to be used for creating containers. Our web service uses the build property to instruct Compose to build our custom image from a Dockerfile. However, to use a preexisting image instead, we can specify the image's name with the image property. Here we specify the redis image, just like in our docker run command.

Other than this, the main difference is what we *don't* specify.

We don't publish any ports. Our web service needs a published port so that web requests made on our local machine will reach the Rails server, running inside a container. Redis, however, doesn't need to be accessed externally; in fact, for security, we'd prefer it wasn't. By not exposing a port, it's hidden and inaccessible to the outside world.

We also don't specify any volumes to be mounted. The web service used volumes to mount our local directory containing our Rails project code inside the container. We did this so that, as we edit the files locally, the changes are automatically picked up inside the container too. For Redis, we don't need this behavior—we're not modifying any files.

Now, let's start our Redis server:

```
$ docker-compose up -d redis
```

We can see Redis starting up by viewing the logs:

```
$ docker-compose logs redis
Attaching to myapp_redis_1
redis_1  | 1:C 15 Jan 2019 10:03:52.794 # oO0o00Oo0000o Redis is starting oO
0Oo0OOo0OO0o
redis_1  | 1:C 15 Jan 2019 10:03:52.794 # Redis version=5.0.3, bits=64,
commit=00000000, modified=0, pid=1, just started
«...»
redis_1  | 1:M 15 Jan 2019 10:03:52.796 * Running mode=standalone, port=6379
«...»
redis_1  | 1:M 15 Jan 2019 10:03:52.796 # Server initialized
«...»
redis_1  | 1:M 15 Jan 2019 10:03:52.796 * Ready to accept connections
```

Great! We've successfully set up Redis as a new service for our application.

Manually Connecting to the Redis Server

We've just started Redis using Compose and saw from the output that it was running. However, since we're still getting familiar with Docker, let's manually connect to the Redis server and interact with it to prove to ourselves it really does work.

A quick way to do this is using the Redis command-line interface (redis-cli). We can leverage the same redis image, which already has redis-cli installed. Handy.

Rather than having to set up a new, separate service in Compose, we can piggyback on the existing redis service, since it uses the redis image we need. Using what we learned in *Running One-Off Commands*, on page 54, we can run redis-cli and connect to our Redis server with the following command:

```
$ docker-compose run --rm redis redis-cli -h redis
```

This command says, "In a throwaway container (--rm) for the redis service, run the command redis-cli -h redis." On running it, you should see the standard Redis prompt showing the hostname and port it's running on:

```
redis:6379>
```

Feel free to play around. For example, try running the ping command, which should give you the "PONG" response. When you're done, exit with the command quit—this will terminate the Redis client and, as a result, the container.

So there you have it. Our Redis server is up and running, and we can connect to it from a separate container. Note that we're using docker-compose run—rather than exec—specifically so that the redis-cli runs in a new, separate container, albeit based on the same redis image. This shows that we're able to access the Redis server from a *different* container.

But, hang on a sec! Aren't containers supposed to be isolated? How come we were able to connect from the container running redis-cli to the container running the redis server?

Good question. Let's explore this in the next section.

How Containers Can Talk to Each Other

If two containers are isolated, independent processes, how come, as we just saw, that they are able to talk to one another? While it's true that the *code and processes* running in a container are sandboxed, that does not mean the container has no way to communicate with the outside world. If containers could not communicate, we would not be able to connect them together to create a powerful, connected system of services that together make up our application.

If you remember back to *Launching Our App*, on page 47, we said that docker-compose up creates a new network for the app. By default, all containers for our app are connected to the app's network and can communicate with each other. This means that our containers, just like a physical or virtual server, can communicate outside themselves using TCP/IP networking.

Let's list our currently defined networks using the command:

```
$ docker network ls
```

You should see some output similar to the following:

```
NETWORK ID        NAME              DRIVER       SCOPE
128925dfad81      bridge            bridge       local
5bd7167263e8      host              host         local
e2af02026928      myapp_default     bridge       local
d1145155d62a      none              null         local
```

The first network called bridge is a legacy network to provide backwards compatibility with some older Docker features—we won't be using it now that we've switched to Compose. Similarly, the host and none networks are special networks that Docker sets up that we don't need to care about.

The network we do care about is called myapp_default—this is our app's dedicated network that Compose created for us (Compose uses the <appname>_default naming convention). The reason Compose creates this network for us is simple: it knows that the services we're defining are all related to the same application, so inevitably they are going to need to talk to one another.

But how do containers on this network find each other?

All Docker networks (except for the legacy bridge network) have built-in Domain Name System (DNS) name resolution. That means that we can communicate with other containers running on the same network by name. Compose uses the service name (as defined in our docker-compose.yml) as the DNS entry. So if we wanted to reach our web service, that's accessible via the hostname web. This provides a basic form of *service discovery*—a consistent way of finding container-based services, even across container restarts.

This explains how we were able to connect from the ad-hoc container running the redis-cli to our Redis server running as the redis service. Here's the command we used:

```
$ docker-compose run --rm redis redis-cli -h redis
```

The option -h redis says, "Connect to the host named redis." This only worked because Compose had already created our app's network and set up DNS entries for each service. In particular, our redis service can be referred to by the hostname redis.

Our Rails App Talking to Redis

Although it's great that we've started up a Redis server using Compose, it's not much use to us by itself. The whole point of running the Redis server is so our Rails app can talk to it and use it as a key-value store. So let's connect our Rails app to Redis and actually use it for something. Sound like fun?

Now, there are a million ways an app might want to use Redis. For our purposes, though, we don't really care *what* we use Redis for; we care more about *how* to use it. We're going to use an intentionally basic example: our Rails app will simply store and retrieve a value. However, keep the larger point in mind—once you know how to set up the Rails app to talk to the Redis server in a container, you can use it however you like.

Ready? Let's begin.

Installing the Redis Gem

The first thing we need to do to get our Rails app talking to Redis is to install the redis gem. You may remember that to update our gems, we need to update our image as we saw on page 55.

So first, in our Gemfile, uncomment the Redis gem in the Gemfile like so:

```
gem 'redis', '~> 4.0'
```

Next, stop our Rails server:

```
$ docker-compose stop web
```

and rebuild our custom Rails image:

```
$ docker-compose build web
```

Among other things, this runs bundle install, which installs the Redis gem:

```
Building web
Step 1/8 : FROM ruby:2.6
«...»
Step 6/8 : RUN bundle install
«...»
Installing redis 4.1.0
«...»
Bundle complete! 16 Gemfile dependencies, 69 gems now installed.
Bundled gems are installed into `/usr/local/bundle`
«...»
Removing intermediate container 3831c10d2cb5
 ---> 1ca01125bd35
Step 7/8 : COPY . /usr/src/app/
 ---> 852dc1f2b419
Step 8/8 : CMD ["bin/rails", "s", "-b", "0.0.0.0"]
 ---> Running in 280c7e2eb556
Removing intermediate container 280c7e2eb556
 ---> d9b3e5325308
Successfully built d9b3e5325308
Successfully tagged myapp_web:latest
```

It's good to get into the habit of rebuilding our image to perform bundle install for us, having updated our Gemfile. That said, we'll learn about a more advanced approach to gem management on page 113 that, as well as being much faster, allows us to stick with our familiar bundle install workflow.

Let's start up our newly built Rails server again:

```
$ docker-compose up -d web
```

Updating Our Rails App to Use Redis

Next, we're going to actually use Redis from our Rails app. As we said before, we just want a basic demonstration that we can connect to the Redis server and store and retrieve values. So let's start by generating a welcome controller in our Rails app with a single index action:

Linux Users: File Ownership

 Make sure you have chowned the files by running:

```
$ sudo chown <your_user>:<your_group> -R .
```

See *File Ownership and Permissions*, on page 199, for more details.

```
$ docker-compose exec web bin/rails g controller welcome index
      create  app/controllers/welcome_controller.rb
       route  get 'welcome/index'
      invoke  erb
      create    app/views/welcome
      create    app/views/welcome/index.html.erb
      invoke  helper
      create    app/helpers/welcome_helper.rb
      invoke  assets
      invoke    coffee
      create      app/assets/javascripts/welcome.coffee
      invoke    scss
      create      app/assets/stylesheets/welcome.scss
```

Let's modify our welcome#index action (in app/controllers/welcome_controller.rb) to be as follows:

```
Line 1  class WelcomeController < ApplicationController
     2    def index
     3      redis = Redis.new(host: "redis", port: 6379)
     4      redis.incr "page hits"
     5
     6      @page_hits = redis.get "page hits"
     7    end
     8  end
```

In our index action, on line 3, we use the Redis client gem to connect to the Redis server by name and by the port number we expect it to be running on. Then, on line 4, we increment a Redis key-value pair, called "page hits." If you're wondering what happens the very first time this code is run, don't fret: if the key is not found, Redis will initialize it to zero, so our code will work as expected. Finally, on line 6, we fetch the current number of page hits from Redis, storing it in an instance variable, ready to display it in our view.

Now let's edit our view file (app/views/welcome/index.html.erb) to display the number of page hits:

```
<h1>This page has been viewed <%= pluralize(@page_hits, 'time') %>!</h1>
```

Finally, in config/routes.rb, let's change the autogenerated route so we can access our new WelcomeController's index action from /welcome (rather than /welcome/index):

```
Rails.application.routes.draw do
  get 'welcome', to: 'welcome#index'
end
```

Now let's visit our Rails app in the browser at http://localhost:3000/welcome. You should see a page with our rendered welcome index.html.erb file, as shown in the following figure:

This page has been viewed 1 time!

The page loads without errors—a good sign. Now try reloading the page. Every time you do, you should see the number of page hits increasing.

What does this mean? It means that our Rails app connected to the Redis server, incremented the value of "page hits" from default of 0 to 1, and finally displayed our welcome message with the number of page hits. More generally, we successfully got two containers to talk to each other. This is possible thanks to Compose creating the network for the app and automatically attaching containers to it.

Starting the Entire App with Docker Compose

We've just added Redis as a new service to our Compose file and configured our Rails app to talk to it. As we did this, the Rails server was already running, so we started the Redis server by itself with docker-compose run redis. However, one of the beauties of Compose is that no matter how many services we add to our application, we can manage it, in its entirety, with a single command, replacing the need for gems like Foreman.[3]

We can stop both the Rails server and Redis server in one go with:

```
$ docker-compose stop
```

You can verify that both services are stopped by running:

```
$ docker-compose ps
```

You should see something like this:

```
Name              Command                     State     Ports
-------------------------------------------------------------------
myapp_redis_1     docker-entrypoint.sh redis ...   Exit 0
myapp_web_1       bin/rails s -b 0.0.0.0           Exit 1
```

---

3. https://rubygems.org/gems/foreman

This shows that both Redis and our web service have stopped; the State column says Exit along with the status code the command terminated with (your exit status may be different). If, for some reason, either are still running, stop them with the docker-compose stop (or kill) command.

Now let's start up the entire app again—both the Rails server *and* Redis:

```
$ docker-compose up -d
```

Now if we run:

```
$ docker-compose ps
```

we can see both services are running:

```
Name                Command                   State    Ports
-------------------------------------------------------------------------
myapp_redis_1   docker-entrypoint.sh redis…   Up       6379/tcp
myapp_web_1     bin/rails s -b 0.0.0.0        Up       0.0.0.0:3000->3000/tcp
```

Now, the moment of truth. Is our welcome#index action still connecting to the Redis server? Browse to http://localhost:3000/welcome again (or refresh the page if it's still open), and you should see the following familiar screen (but with the hit counter continuing to increase):

This page has been viewed 2 times!

Quick Recap

The true power of using containers for our apps is not running a process in an individual container (though that's useful), but rather how we're able to wire containers together so they can talk to each other.

In this chapter, we've seen how we can add services to our application, running in separate containers. More importantly, we've seen how Docker's built-in networking is used to let the services talk to each other.

Let's review the highlights:

1. We started a Redis server in a container, using docker run. We covered two new options: --name for giving containers a human-friendly name, and -d for running a container in detached mode.

2. We added a separate service in Compose for running the Redis server.

3. We verified that the Redis server was running (and that we could connect to it from a separate container) by starting a new container to run redis-cli.

4. We discussed the networking features Docker provides, and how Compose facilitates containers talking to each other.

5. We connected our Rails app to the Redis server, making it store and increment a value, which we then retrieved and displayed.

6. Finally, we saw that our trusty docker-compose up just works, and will start up both the Rails *and* Redis servers in one go.

Next, we're going to take what we've learned about Compose and use it to add a Postgres database. We'll go a step further and see how to ensure our data persists even if the container running our database were deleted.

## CHAPTER 6

Adding a Database: Postgres

I don't know about you, but I'm feeling great about our progress. We've gradually been leveling up our skills and are now within touching distance of our Dockerized Rails app having all the capabilities we're used to when running Rails locally.

However, there's still one glaring omission: we haven't set up a database. The vast majority of Rails applications require some persistent storage.

In this chapter, we'll rectify that, building on our experience of adding the Redis server, to connect a Postgres database.

While reading this chapter, remember to keep the bigger picture in mind. The skills you're learning apply to *any* services you might want to add to your app, be it running background jobs (such as Sidekiq), Elasticsearch, or a JavaScript front end for a Rails API.

Starting a Postgres Server

We want to run a Postgres server for our Rails app to use. The process is very similar to how we added Redis.

In the previous chapter, we started by familiarizing ourselves with how to run the Redis server with docker run. However, now that we've had some experience with adding a service, let's take the safety wheels off and jump straight to setting up Postgres directly with Compose.

Let's add Postgres to our docker-compose.yml file:

```
version: '3'
services:
  web:
    build: .
    ports:
      - "3000:3000"
    volumes:
      - .:/usr/src/app
  redis:
    image: redis
➤ database:
➤   image: postgres
➤   environment:
➤     POSTGRES_USER: postgres
➤     POSTGRES_PASSWORD: some-long-secure-password
➤     POSTGRES_DB: myapp_development
```

We've defined a new database service using the official postgres image.[1] We're relying on this image's default CMD instruction—CMD ["postgres"]—which starts the Postgres server.[2]

As with redis, our new database service has no need for port mappings or volumes. We don't want the database to be accessible externally to our application, and we don't need to mount any files into the Postgres container.

We do, however, specify a new property called environment. You may well be able to guess what this does: it tells Docker to set the subsequent environment variables inside the container. Here, we're specifying that POSTGRES_USER should be set to postgres; POSTGRES_PASSWORD should be set to some-long-secure-password; and POSTGRES_DB should be set to myapp_development.

Why do we set these?

Just like the non-Dockerized version of Postgres allows you to specify certain parameters as environment variables,[3] the same is true for the Dockerized version.[4] When Postgres launches, if POSTGRES_USER is set, its value will be used as the name of the superuser account. Similarly, if POSTGRES_PASSWORD is set, this will be used as the superuser password. Finally, if POSTGRES_DB is set, this will be used as the name of the default database that's created on launch.

---

1. https://hub.docker.com/_/postgres/
2. https://github.com/docker-library/postgres/blob/674466e0d47517f4e05ec2025ae996e71b26cae9/10/Dockerfile#L133
3. https://www.postgresql.org/docs/9.1/static/libpq-envars.html
4. https://hub.docker.com/_/postgres/

It's not ideal to have our database password in the docker-compose.yml file: this file should be committed to version control, but it's a security risk to commit files containing secrets. We'll revisit this shortly. Also, technically, we didn't need to set POSTGRES_USER since we're setting its default value. However, I've included it because it's good practice to make things configurable.[5]

OK. With our docker-compose.yml updated, we can start Postgres:

```
$ docker-compose up -d database
```

We're starting our database service in detached mode. We can verify it's up and running with:

```
$ docker-compose ps
        Name              Command          State      Ports
-------------------------------------------------------------------------
myapp_database_1   docker-entrypoint.sh pos…   Up    5432/tcp
myapp_redis_1      docker-entrypoint.sh red…   Up    6379/tcp
myapp_web_1        bin/rails s -b 0.0.0.0      Up    0.0.0.0:3000->3000/tcp
```

We now have three containers for our app, and we can see that our new addition—the database—is running.

As a further check, we can view the database container's output:

```
$ docker-compose logs database
Attaching to myapp_database_1
«...»
database_1  | PostgreSQL init process complete; ready for start up.
database_1  |
database_1  | 2019-01-15 10:07:29.394 UTC [1] LOG: listening on IPv4 address
"0.0.0.0", port 5432
database_1  | 2019-01-15 10:07:29.394 UTC [1] LOG: listening on IPv6 address
"::", port 5432
database_1  | 2019-01-15 10:07:29.397 UTC [1] LOG: listening on Unix socket
"/var/run/postgresql/.s.PGSQL.5432"
database_1  | 2019-01-15 10:07:29.409 UTC [60] LOG:  database system was shut
down at 2019-01-15 10:07:29 UTC
database_1  | 2019-01-15 10:07:29.414 UTC [1] LOG:  database system is ready
to accept connections
```

Remember that this command shows the *container's* logs—that is, its output rather than Postgres' log file output.

---

5.   https://12factor.net/config

Connecting to Postgres from a Separate Container

As you become more and more comfortable with using Compose, you'll find that you trust it to do what you need. A quick docker-compose ps is probably all you need to verify a service is running (sometimes you may even skip that).

However, since running services like Postgres inside a container is still fairly new for us, let's take the extra step of manually connecting to it from a different container, just like we did with Redis. While learning, for me at least, this helps build my confidence in the tools.

As was the case with Redis, the postgres image comes preinstalled with psql—the Postgres client. This means we can piggyback on our new database service in order to run a one-off container, based on the postgres image. However, instead of using the default command for the image, which starts the Postgres *server*, we instead run a command to start the Postgres *client*.

We can do this by running the following command:

```
$ docker-compose run --rm database psql -U postgres -h database
```

Here we're saying, "Start a new, throwaway container (run --rm) for the database service and run the command psql -u postgres -h database inside it." This command starts the Postgres client, telling it to connect to the hostname database with the postgres user. We're relying on the fact that Compose magically sets up a network for our application with DNS configured so that the hostname database will reach the container running our database service.

We could have used exec instead of run --rm, which would have avoided starting a new container and, instead, executed the command on the database container that's already running. However, we deliberately wanted the extra verification of connecting from a different container.

When you run this command, you'll be prompted to enter a password:

```
Password for user postgres:
```

Go ahead and enter some-long-secure-password—the password we set in our docker-compose.yml file. This should be accepted and take you to the psql prompt:

```
psql (11.1 (Debian 11.1-1.pgdg90+1))
Type "help" for help.

postgres=#
```

Excellent. We're connected to our database service, running Postgres, and have proven that everything is working as we hoped. When you're ready, you can quit the psql client as follows by typing \q <Enter>.

Connecting Our Rails App to Postgres

We've just seen that our database is up and running and reachable from other containers in our app's network. However, before we can start making use of it, we have to configure our Rails app to connect to it.

Let's do this now.

Installing the Postgres Gem

First things first. In order to get our Rails app talking to Postgres, we need to install the Postgres client gem. Open up your Gemfile and update it to replace:

```
gem 'sqlite3'
```

with:

```
gem 'pg', '~> 1.0'
```

To actually install the new gem, we need to run bundle install, which we do by rebuilding our image (we discuss gem management further on page 113). Let's first stop our Rails server:

```
$ docker-compose stop web
```

and then rebuild our image:

```
$ docker-compose build web
Building web
Step 1/8 : FROM ruby:2.6
«...»
Step 6/8 : RUN bundle install
«...»
Installing pg 1.1.4 with native extensions
«...»
Bundle complete! 16 Gemfile dependencies, 69 gems now installed.
Bundled gems are installed into `/usr/local/bundle`
«...»
Removing intermediate container 9b01b1fa29fc
 ---> f9e6330d40b6
Step 7/8 : COPY . /usr/src/app/
 ---> 70fb0e2e0091
Step 8/8 : CMD ["bin/rails", "s", "-b", "0.0.0.0"]
 ---> Running in 16cc0923b855
Removing intermediate container 16cc0923b855
 ---> d4ffbe8f72d3
Successfully built d4ffbe8f72d3
Successfully tagged myapp_web:latest
```

With the Postgres gem installed, we can move on to configuring our database.yml.

Creating Our App Databases

When we created our Rails project, we did so with the default settings, which assumed we were using sqlite for our database. Now that we're setting up Postgres instead, the generated database.yml file is not correct. We need to change it to something more suitable.

Let's open up config/database.yml in an editor and replace its contents with the following Postgres configuration:

```
default: &default
  adapter: postgresql
  encoding: unicode
  host:     <%= ENV.fetch('DATABASE_HOST') %>
  username: <%= ENV.fetch('POSTGRES_USER') %>
  password: <%= ENV.fetch('POSTGRES_PASSWORD') %>
  database: <%= ENV.fetch('POSTGRES_DB') %>
  pool: 5
  variables:
    statement_timeout: 5000

development:
  <<: *default

test:
  <<: *default
  database: myapp_test

production:
  <<: *default
```

Hopefully, this all looks pretty familiar to you.

We're specifying the most important config (host, username, password, and database) via environment variables. Generally this is considered a good practice,[6] although, as we'll see later, Docker provides an even more secure approach. Currently, though, these environment variables are not set for our web service.

Let's fix that. We have to update our docker-compose.yml to ensure these variables are set in our Rails app container, like so:

```
version: '3'

services:

  web:
    build: .
    ports:
      - "3000:3000"
```

---

6.   https://12factor.net/config

```
   volumes:
     - .:/usr/src/app
➤  environment:
➤    DATABASE_HOST: database
➤    POSTGRES_USER: postgres
➤    POSTGRES_PASSWORD: some-long-secure-password
➤    POSTGRES_DB: myapp_development
 redis:
   image: redis
 database:
   image: postgres
   environment:
     POSTGRES_USER: postgres
     POSTGRES_PASSWORD: some-long-secure-password
     POSTGRES_DB: myapp_development
```

In the pre-Docker world, we'd normally set DATABASE_HOST to localhost since the database would be running on our local machine. Here, though, we specify the name of our service that runs Postgres: database. This resolves to our database service's containers thanks to DNS provided by our app's network.

We also set the POSTGRES_USER, POSTGRES_PASSWORD, and POSTGRES_DB environment variables to match those set for the database service; this means our web service will have the correct credentials to log into the database.

This should now work, but notice that we now have quite a lot of environment variables, and two are duplicated across the web and database services. We also said we'd rather not include secrets in our docker-compose.yml file so we can commit it to our source repo. Let's kill two birds with one stone and extract the environment variables into separate files.

First, let's create some directories to store our environment-specific config:

```
$ mkdir -p .env/development
```

Then create the file .env/development/web (without a file extension), which contains our web-service-specific environment variables:

```
DATABASE_HOST=database
```

and another file, .env/development/database, containing those for our database service:

```
POSTGRES_USER=postgres
POSTGRES_PASSWORD=some-long-secure-password
POSTGRES_DB=myapp_development
```

Now we need to tell Compose to use these files instead of explicitly setting the variables directly. We do this using the env_file directive:

```
version: '3'
services:

  web:
    build: .
    ports:
      - "3000:3000"
    volumes:
      - .:/usr/src/app
➤   env_file:
➤     - .env/development/database
➤     - .env/development/web

  redis:
    image: redis

  database:
    image: postgres
➤   env_file:
➤     - .env/development/database
```

We could have named the environment files anything we liked, but I chose a simple naming scheme that makes sense. Similarly, you are free to use whatever file structure and naming conventions you like for the environment variable files (currently under .env), so long as you refer to them correctly in the Compose file.

With this small refactor done, we're ready to create our development and test databases using the standard Rails command bin/rails db:create, targeting the command at our web service:

```
$ docker-compose run --rm web bin/rails db:create
```

In this case, we used run --rm rather than exec because the currently running web container won't have the newly added environment variables set until we restart. The new, throwaway container that runs this command will.

You should see the following output showing our databases have been created successfully:

```
Database 'myapp_development' already exists
Created database 'myapp_test'
```

You'll notice that the myapp_development database already exists, which is a bit strange since this is the first time we've said to create it. That's because the postgres image will automatically create a default database when it's first started; if set, it uses the value of the POSTGRES_DB environment variable as the name for this table. In our case, that's myapp_development, which is why the table already exists.

Great, we're almost there.

Restarting the Rails Server

Having set up Rails to use our Postgres database running in a container and created the databases, the final step is to start up our Rails server with the new config and environment variables. However, because Compose will just reuse existing containers for a server, we have to explicitly tell it to recreate the container for our web service.

Here's how we do that:

```
$ docker-compose up -d --force-recreate web
```

The --force-recreate says, "Recreate the service's containers."

Now, go ahead and visit http://localhost:3000 to verify the app is connected to Postgres; if all is well, you'll see the standard Rails start screen, whereas ActiveRecord will raise a PG::ConnectionBad error if it can't connect.

That's it—we're up and running with Postgres.

Yay! You're on Rails!

```
Rails version: 5.2.2
Ruby version: 2.6.0 (x86_64-linux)
```

Using the Database in Practice

We know that, having configured our Rails app to talk to our Postgres database, our Rails app started successfully; however, we're relying on the *absence of an error* as proof that the database is connected correctly. While, technically, that's all we need, let's make sure it's working as expected by interacting with the database from our app. This will also give us more practice at developing our Rails app with Docker, via the Compose CLI.

Let's generate a basic UsersController in our Rails app. For the sake of speed, we're going to just use Rail's generate scaffold command:

```
$ docker-compose exec web \
    bin/rails g scaffold User first_name:string last_name:string
      invoke  active_record
      create    db/migrate/20190115100954_create_users.rb
      create    app/models/user.rb
      invoke  resource_route
       route    resources :users
      invoke  scaffold_controller
      create    app/controllers/users_controller.rb
      invoke    erb
      create      app/views/users
      create      app/views/users/index.html.erb
      create      app/views/users/edit.html.erb
      create      app/views/users/show.html.erb
      create      app/views/users/new.html.erb
      «...»
```

Linux Users: File Ownership

Remember to chown the files we've just generated by running the following command:

```
$ sudo chown <your_user>:<your_group> -R .
```

See *File Ownership and Permissions*, on page 199, for more details.

Now we need to run the migrations to create the Users table. You should be starting to get comfortable with running standard Rails commands targeted against our web service using Compose, just like this:

```
$ docker-compose exec web bin/rails db:migrate
== 20190115100954 CreateUsers: migrating ====================================
-- create_table(:users)
   -> 0.0585s
== 20190115100954 CreateUsers: migrated (0.0587s) ===========================
```

OK, we should be good to go—let's try this out. With the app still running, navigate to http://localhost:3000/users in a browser. You should see the familiar Rails scaffold for creating and listing users as shown in the following figure. Make sure you can create and delete users.

Users

First name Last name

New User

Great, we have Postgres all set up with Compose.

Decoupling Data from the Container

It's great that we've set up our database so we can persist data in our Rails app. However, currently, there's a major failing in how it works. Let's see what the problem is, and see how to get around it.

Part of the philosophy of using Docker is that we should treat containers as ephemeral—throwaway things that we spin up, use, and then delete. However, our Postgres database is running in a container and persisting our data by writing and modifying files *on disk* inside the container. What happens to our data if we delete our database container? Yep, you've guessed it: we say bye bye to all our lovely data. Not really what we want.

Now that we're going to be storing important data in our database, we need to think a bit more carefully about this.

Just like in our code where we try to decouple things that change frequently from things that don't, we want to decouple our *data* from the containers that generate and use it. Our data should be stored *separately* from the container running the database. That way, we could delete, remove, and recreate the container without affecting the data.

The answer: we store persistent data in volumes, which by their very nature are decoupled from the life cycle of containers. Even if we delete a container with a connected volume, the volume continues to exist independently, storing our data safely. We can then recreate the container, hooking up the volume, and everything is hunky-dory.

Docker allows us to create a few different types of volumes, all of which would do the job. For example, we've already seen how to mount a local volume. However, there's another type of volume better suited to our purpose. We don't really care *where* or *how* the files are stored, we just care that they *are* stored somewhere separately. For this, we can create a *named volume*: a self-contained *bucket* of file storage, completely managed by Docker.

But enough of the theory; let's see how we do this in practice.

Named volumes can be created and managed through the docker volume command. While that's worth knowing about, since we're using Compose, we can let it handle the management of the volumes for us.

Here's our docker-compose.yml modified to store our persistent data on a volume:

```
Line 1  version: '3'

     -  services:

     5    web:
     -      build: .
     -      ports:
     -        - "3000:3000"
     -      volumes:
    10        - .:/usr/src/app
     -      env_file:
     -        - .env/development/database
     -        - .env/development/web

    15    redis:
     -      image: redis

     -    database:
     -      image: postgres
    20      env_file:
     -        - .env/development/database
     -      volumes:
     -        - db_data:/var/lib/postgresql/data

    25 volumes:
     -    db_data:
```

The first step is to tell Compose that we need a named volume. Named volumes are defined under the top-level volumes property (line 25); here, we've defined a named volume called db_data (line 26).

Next, we need to tell Compose to mount the named volume inside our database container, using the familiar volumes property (line 22). Mounting a named volume (line 23) is similar to mounting a local directory (line 10)—the difference is that the part before the colon refers to the name of the named volume rather than a local path. Here (line 23) we're saying, "Mount the db_data named volume at /var/lib/postgresql/data"—the directory where the Postgres image stores its database files that we want to persist.[7]

OK, let's give this a whirl. We've changed our Compose definition for our database service, so that's the one we need to restart. However, again, because Compose reuses the same container for a service unless we tell it otherwise, we have to explicitly tell Compose to recreate the database container to pick up our new volume settings.

First stop the database service:

```
$ docker-compose stop database
```

Then let's explicitly remove its container:

```
$ docker-compose rm -f database
```

Compose would normally ask us to confirm before removing the container—the force (-f) option tells it to just go ahead and do it.

OK, it's time to bring our database back up:

```
$ docker-compose up -d database
Creating volume "myapp_db_data" with default driver
Creating myapp_database_1 ... done
```

Since our new volume is now mounted in the container, we've wiped any previous databases and data we had stored, so we'll need to recreate and migrate the databases.

Let's do this now:

```
$ docker-compose exec web bin/rails db:create db:migrate
Database 'myapp_development' already exists
Created database 'myapp_test'
== 20190115100954 CreateUsers: migrating ===================================
-- create_table(:users)
   -> 0.0127s
== 20190115100954 CreateUsers: migrated (0.0143s) ==========================
```

OK, now let's make sure our app is still working. Visit http://localhost:3000/users in the browser, and make sure you see our User scaffold. Great—the volume seems to be working.

---

7. https://hub.docker.com/_/postgres/

Let's prove that our data is now persisted even if we delete the database container. First, we need to store some data: add one or more users through the Rails scaffold. In the following figure, I've created a single user for myself.

Users

First name Last name

Rob   Isenberg   Show **Edit** Destroy

New User

Now that we have some data stored, let's stop the database container:

```
$ docker-compose stop database
Stopping myapp_database_1 ... done
```

and then delete it (you will need to confirm when asked):

```
$ docker-compose rm database
Going to remove myapp_database_1
Are you sure? [yN] y
Removing myapp_database_1 ... done
```

Next, we recreate it and start it up with:

```
$ docker-compose up -d database
```

If this works, we should see our user data, exactly as it was before we deleted the database container. Reload the browser (at http://localhost:3000/users), and…our data is still there. Hurrah!

But Where Actually Is My Data?

We said that Docker manages an area of the filesystem for named volumes, but where actually is it? We can find out where our db_data named volume (which Compose prefixes with our app folder to become myapp_db_data) is located by running:

```
$ docker volume inspect --format '{{ .Mountpoint }}' myapp_db_data
/var/lib/docker/volumes/myapp_db_data/_data
```

As we can see, named volumes are stored in /var/lib/docker/volumes/.[8] On Linux, this will be a path on the local filesystem, but on macOS or Windows, this refers to the path *inside* the Dockerhost VM.

---

8.   https://docs.docker.com/storage/#choose-the-right-type-of-mount

Quick Recap

In this chapter, we learned how to set up and configure a database for our Rails app—something the vast majority of Rails apps typically need.

Let's review what we covered:

- We started up a Postgres server in a container using Compose.

- We verified that the Postgres server was running by connecting with the Postgres client from a separate container.

- We configured our Rails app to talk to Postgres by installing the Postgres gem, modifying our database.yml file, and running the Rake task to create the databases.

- We put our new database through its paces by generating a scaffold, running migrations, and inserting, deleting, and updating records.

- We discussed why it's a good idea to decouple our database container from data we want to persist.

- Finally, we used a named volume to store our data separately, allowing us to manage its life cycle independently of the container.

You've now seen how to add two services: Redis and Postgres. You should be able to apply this same knowledge to add any other services you can think of. In fact, we'll add yet another service in the next chapter, as we turn our attention away from back-end technologies to explore how to incorporate a modern, JavaScript front end for your Rails app.

## CHAPTER 7

Playing Nice with JavaScript

We're living in a JavaScript renaissance—no longer is it the whipping boy of language purists. Rails has embraced modern JavaScript technologies like React through its inclusion of Webpacker: a gem that brings webpack support.

As Rails developers, it's important to be able to incorporate these technologies into our apps as needed, so our Docker environment needs to support us in that endeavor.

In this chapter, we'll explore the options for working with JavaScript as part of our Rails development. We'll also see how to include a React front end in our Rails app by installing and configuring Webpacker.

By the end of this chapter, our Docker-based development environment will play nice with all this modern JavaScript goodness.

The JavaScript Front-End Options

There are a number of different options when it comes to combining JavaScript into the front end for your Rails apps. Perhaps the biggest choice is whether your Rails app will serve up the front end or not. Both are equally valid options, and each way has some advantages and disadvantages and will lead to different setups.

If your Rails app is not serving up your front end, that means you're using your Rails app as an API layer. In this case, you'd have a separate front end, typically written purely in JavaScript, whether that's React, Ember, Vue.js, or something else. This scenario is outside the scope of the book, since it involves getting very JavaScript-specific with your setup. However, in general terms, it's quite straightforward, and you will largely be applying the skills you've already learned.

Here's a basic outline:

- *Rename your web service.* Naming is important. In this scenario, your Rails app is really the API or back end, so you should name it as such.

- *Create a custom image for running your JavaScript front-end app.* In the same way we've created a custom image to run our Rails app, you would do the same but for your JS front end. Its Dockerfile could build on top of a standard Node.js image,[1] adding the app-specific setup required.

- *Create a separate, front-end service in your docker-compose.yml.* This would be your standalone JavaScript application. You would configure, via environment variables, the API endpoint it should use (the domain name and port of the Rails API).

If, on the other hand, you're using Rails to serve up your front end, that means using the facilities that Rails provides. Rails offers two mechanisms for serving up JavaScript front ends: the (Sprockets-based) asset pipeline or the new Webpacker approach added in Rails 5.1.

The traditional Sprockets-based asset pipeline works out of the box without any special setup. As part of running the Rails server, your assets will automatically be compiled and served up in your views in the standard Rails way. We'll see an example of this in the upcoming testing chapter on page 95.

Getting your Rails app working with Webpacker takes a little bit more setup with Docker. Since this is such a popular approach, we're going to guide you through how to set this up throughout the rest of the chapter.

Rails JavaScript Front End with Webpacker

Rails has included a way to build rich JavaScript front ends into your apps since version 5.1, using a gem called webpacker. Webpacker has a modular architecture, allowing you to integrate different front-end technologies, be it React, Ember, Vue.js, or even Elm.

Using React as an example, let's see how we'd configure Webpacker in our Dockerized app.

First things first. Webpacker requires Yarn and a current version of Node. This requires an update to our Docker image:

```
Line 1  FROM ruby:2.6
   -    LABEL maintainer="rob@DockerForRailsDevelopers.com"
   -
```

---

1. https://hub.docker.com/_/node/

```
      # Allow apt to work with https-based sources
  5   RUN apt-get update -yqq && apt-get install -yqq --no-install-recommends \
        apt-transport-https

      # Ensure we install an up-to-date version of Node
      # See https://github.com/yarnpkg/yarn/issues/2888
 10   RUN curl -sL https://deb.nodesource.com/setup_8.x | bash -

      # Ensure latest packages for Yarn
      RUN curl -sS https://dl.yarnpkg.com/debian/pubkey.gpg | apt-key add -
      RUN echo "deb https://dl.yarnpkg.com/debian/ stable main" | \
 15     tee /etc/apt/sources.list.d/yarn.list

      # Install packages
      RUN apt-get update -yqq && apt-get install -yqq --no-install-recommends \
        nodejs \
 20     yarn

      COPY Gemfile* /usr/src/app/
      WORKDIR /usr/src/app
      RUN bundle install
 25
      COPY . /usr/src/app/

      CMD ["bin/rails", "s", "-b", "0.0.0.0"]
```

To install an up-to-date version of Yarn, we have to add Yarn's Debian package repository to the list of sources (lines 13–15). However, since Yarn's package repo uses HTTPS, we have to install the apt-transport-https package (lines 5–6) to allow this to work.

Unfortunately, there's a dependency issue between Yarn and the (old) version of Node.js installed by default. We solve this on line 10 by adding Node's package repository to the list of sources; this ensures we install a more up-to-date version of Node.

Finally, on line 20, we add yarn to the list of packages we install. With yarn and an up-to-date version of Node installed, we're now ready to configure our app to use Webpacker.

Had we known we were going to be using Webpacker when first creating our app, we could have included support using the --webpack option—for example:

```
$ rails new myapp --webpack=react <other options>
```

The --webpack=react option would have generated our app with support for React out of the box. However, having already generated our app, adding Webpacker support requires a couple of manual steps.

We first have to update our Gemfile to include the Webpacker gem:

```
gem 'webpacker', '~> 3.5'
```

Then we run bundle install via rebuilding our image:

```
$ docker-compose build web
```

Let's stop the web service because it's currently running our old version without the Webpacker gem installed:

```
$ docker-compose stop web
```

Now we can install Webpacker in our app:

```
$ docker-compose run web bin/rails webpacker:install
```

---

inotify Overflow Error

Unfortunately, when running the previous command, you may encounter the following error message, which appears to be caused by a bug in the rb-inotify gem:[2]

```
run() in thread failed: inotify event queue has overflowed.
```

Although unsightly, it doesn't seem to have any material impact, and you can safely ignore it.

---

followed by the Webpacker React integration:

```
$ docker-compose run web bin/rails webpacker:install:react
```

OK, our app is configured for Webpacker and React. However, before we can truly say we're done, we need a way to compile our React assets automatically.

Compiling Assets with Webpacker

As part of Webpacker, Rails provides the webpack-dev-server binary. This is a small server that runs in the background, automatically compiling our webpack-managed files.

If you were developing locally, this would just be another command you'd issue from your terminal. However, the Docker way is to run this as a separate service in its own container.

Let's add a new service for it to our docker-compose.yml file:

---

2. https://github.com/guard/rb-inotify/issues/61

```
Line 1  version: '3'
    -
    -  services:
    -    web:
    5      build: .
    -      ports:
    -        - "3000:3000"
    -      volumes:
    -        - .:/usr/src/app
   10      env_file:
    -        - .env/development/web
    -        - .env/development/database
    -      environment:
    -        - WEBPACKER_DEV_SERVER_HOST=webpack_dev_server
   15
    -    webpack_dev_server:
    -      build: .
    -      command: ./bin/webpack-dev-server
    -      ports:
   20        - 3035:3035
    -      volumes:
    -        - .:/usr/src/app
    -      env_file:
    -        - .env/development/web
   25        - .env/development/database
    -      environment:
    -        - WEBPACKER_DEV_SERVER_HOST=0.0.0.0
    -
    -    redis:
   30      image: redis
    -
    -    database:
    -      image: postgres
    -      env_file:
   35        - .env/development/database
    -      volumes:
    -        - db_data:/var/lib/postgresql/data
    -
    -  volumes:
   40    db_data:
```

The Rails webpack_dev_server is designed to work in the root of your Rails application; that's why we build from the same Dockerfile (line 17) as our web service.

Although it uses the same image and code, we start our new service with a different command. Instead of starting the Rails server, we run the ./bin/webpack_dev_server command itself (line 18).

We expose the service on webpack-dev-server's default port of 3035 (line 20).

We want the webpack-dev-server to pick up and recompile our changes automatically as we develop locally without having to restart. That's why on line 22, like in our web service, we mount our local files into the container.

The webpack-dev-server command expects to be run with the same configuration as our Rails app. Luckily, having extracted these into files, we can simply reuse the same env_files (lines 23–25).

However, to ensure that webpacker-dev-server responds to requests from any IP address, we set WEBPACKER_DEV_SERVER_HOST to 0.0.0.0 (line 27), much like we did with the Rails server.

Having configured our webpack_dev_server service, we also need to set a Rails environment variable for our web service, so it knows where to find the webpack-dev-server (line 14).

Now we need to start our web service to use our new image and pick up these config changes:

```
$ docker-compose up -d web
```

and then launch our new service:

```
$ docker-compose up -d webpack_dev_server
```

A Hello World React App

Our purpose here is to ensure we can configure our Rails app, using Docker, to allow us to develop modern JavaScript apps using technologies like React. To that end, we just need to show that a simple React app is compiled and loads correctly with our setup.

When we install Webpacker, it adds a sample "Hello World" React app in app/javascript/packs/hello_react.jsx that renders a <div> saying "Hello React!":

```jsx
import React from 'react'
import ReactDOM from 'react-dom'
import PropTypes from 'prop-types'

const Hello = props => (
  <div>Hello {props.name}!</div>
)

Hello.defaultProps = {
  name: 'World'
}
```

```
Hello.propTypes = {
  name: PropTypes.string
}
document.addEventListener('DOMContentLoaded', () => {
  ReactDOM.render(
    <Hello name="React" />,
    document.body.appendChild(document.createElement('div')),
  )
})
```

We're going to use this app to verify Webpacker is set up correctly. First, we need to generate a page that the React app will be loaded on:

```
$ docker-compose exec web bin/rails g controller pages home
      create  app/controllers/pages_controller.rb
       route  get 'pages/home'
      invoke  erb
      create    app/views/pages
      create    app/views/pages/home.html.erb
      invoke  helper
      create    app/helpers/pages_helper.rb
      invoke  assets
      invoke    coffee
      create      app/assets/javascripts/pages.coffee
      invoke    scss
      create      app/assets/stylesheets/pages.scss
```

Let's modify the generated view (app/views/pages/home.html.erb) to load the React app; while we are at it, let's delete the default content and give the page a new title:

```
<%= javascript_pack_tag 'hello_react' %>

<h1>React App</h1>
```

OK, let's try this out. Navigate to http://localhost:3000/pages/home, and you should see the content "Hello React!" displayed on the page. This confirms that our React app is being compiled and loaded correctly.

Auto-updating works too. Update app/javascript/packs/hello_react.jsx to set the defaultProps.name to your name:

```
<Hello name="<Your name>" />
```

Now when you reload the browser, you should see the page has updated (unless your name, coincidentally, is "React").

Thrilling, this app isn't. But with these basics in place, you can now develop with React as part of your Rails app, and build whatever you like.

Quick Recap

That's it—we've finally done it. We now have a fully fledged Rails app running with Docker, fully managed through Compose. It's a thing of beauty, isn't it? Let's quickly recap what we covered in this chapter:

1. We installed Yarn and a more up-to-date version of Node to meet Webpacker's requirements.

2. We installed the Webpacker gem.

3. We added a new service to our docker-compose.yml file that runs the webpack_dev_server to automatically compile our Webpacker JavaScript assets.

4. We created a Hello World React application to verify everything was configured correctly to compile and run a React app.

Now that our app is up and running in all its glory, next we'll turn our attention to setting up and running our tests in a Dockerized environment.

## CHAPTER 8

Testing in a Dockerized Environment

In the previous chapter, we completed our standard app setup by adding a Postgres database. However, we're not quite done with development yet. As professional Ruby developers, we value well-tested code that gives us confidence that we're delivering reliable software. As we rebuild our development environment around Docker, we need to find out how testing fits into the picture. Whatever your personal preferences around testing, it's important to know how to get our testing tools working and playing nice with Docker so that you can use them as needed.

In this chapter, we're going to set up the popular Ruby testing framework: RSpec. I've chosen RSpec over Rails' default—Minitest—for a couple of reasons. First, slightly more effort is needed to set up RSpec, so there's more to learn along the way. Second, it happens to be my testing framework of choice for Rails projects.

That said, if you're an ardent Minitest fan, never fear. It's still worth reading this chapter to continue to build up your familiarity with the Docker commands needed in our normal workflow. Also, the configuration required, especially for Capybara, will be very similar and may largely be translated across to Minitest.

If you've ever set up RSpec on a Rails project before, the majority of what you'll see in this chapter will be very familiar. In fact, squint and you could miss the fact that we're using Docker at all. This is both a testament to how far you've come in your learning and understanding of Docker, and to the fact that, once set up, the Docker tools get out of your way and fade into the background until you need them.

Despite that, this chapter is not without its challenges. There are a few nuances to testing with Docker that we'll tease out. We'll also see that things aren't as straightforward when we get to configuring system specs with Capybara for end-to-end browser testing.

Keep in mind our focus here is not on how to test your code—I'm assuming you're already bringing that knowledge and experience to the table (and if you aren't, there are plenty of good books on the subject[1]). We're just interested in getting some common testing tools set up in a Dockerized environment.

Once more into the breach...

Setting Up RSpec

Now that our app is configured correctly with Compose, setting up RSpec is going to be very familiar. Let's whiz through this quickly.

Following the instructions from rspec-rails,[2] we need to add the following to our Gemfile:

```
group :development, :test do
  # Call 'byebug' anywhere in the code to stop execution and get a debugger…
  gem 'byebug', platforms: [:mri, :mingw, :x64_mingw]
  gem 'rspec-rails', '~> 3.8'
end
```

First, let's stop our web service:

```
$ docker-compose stop web
```

Next, we need to rebuild our image to run bundle install, and then create a new container from it:

```
$ docker-compose build web
Building web
Step 1/12 : FROM ruby:2.6
《...》
Step 7/12 : RUN apt-get update -yqq && apt-get install -yqq --no-install-
recommends   nodejs   yarn
《...》
Bundle complete! 18 Gemfile dependencies, 77 gems now installed.
Bundled gems are installed into `/usr/local/bundle`
《...》
Removing intermediate container dcb3ac9ef4e5
 ---> a1bf00e74754
Step 11/12 : COPY . /usr/src/app/
 ---> 395cd4848b46
Step 12/12 : CMD ["bin/rails", "s", "-b", "0.0.0.0"]
 ---> Running in 47ec46df6236
```

---

1. https://pragprog.com/book/rspec3/effective-testing-with-rspec-3
2. https://github.com/rspec/rspec-rails

```
Removing intermediate container 47ec46df6236
 ---> ea5d358cb673
Successfully built ea5d358cb673
Successfully tagged myapp_web:latest
$ docker-compose up -d --force-recreate web
Recreating myapp_web_1 ... done
```

Next we need to install RSpec, setting up its file structure:

```
$ docker-compose exec web bin/rails generate rspec:install
      create  .rspec
      create  spec
      create  spec/spec_helper.rb
      create  spec/rails_helper.rb
```

With RSpec set up, we're able to run the specs like so:

```
$ docker-compose exec web bin/rails spec
```

However, as you'd expect, this reports that we have no specs currently:

```
No examples found.

Finished in 0.00509 seconds (files took 0.30574 seconds to load)
0 examples, 0 failures
```

Let's take RSpec for a proper test-drive by creating...

Our First Test

Having installed RSpec in our project, it's not very satisfying to see zero tests running. Let's rectify that right now by creating our first test, so that we can see some actual test code running.

Let's generate a spec for our User model:

```
$ docker-compose exec web bin/rails generate rspec:model user
      create  spec/models/user_spec.rb
```

Linux Users: File Ownership

 Remember to chown the files we've generated so you can edit them (see *File Ownership and Permissions*, on page 199):

```
$ sudo chown <your_user>:<your_group> -R .
```

Open the newly created spec/models/user_spec.rb file in your editor. This isn't a book about testing—we just need a basic test to show RSpec is working like we expect. The following should do the trick:

```
require 'rails_helper'

RSpec.describe User do
  describe "validations" do
    it "requires first_name to be set" do
      expect(subject.valid?).to_not be
      expect(subject.errors[:first_name].size).to eq(1)
    end

    it "requires last_name to be set" do
      expect(subject.valid?).to_not be
      expect(subject.errors[:last_name].size).to eq(1)
    end
  end
end
```

Now when we run the tests again:

```
$ docker-compose exec web bin/rails spec
```

we see our specs correctly failing because we haven't implemented any validations on the User model:

```
Failures:

  1) User validations requires first_name to be set
     Failure/Error: expect(subject.valid?).to_not be
       expected true to evaluate to false
     # ./spec/models/user_spec.rb:6:in `block (3 levels) in <top (required)>'

  2) User validations requires last_name to be set
     Failure/Error: expect(subject.valid?).to_not be
       expected true to evaluate to false
     # ./spec/models/user_spec.rb:11:in `block (3 levels) in <top (required)>'

Finished in 0.09403 seconds (files took 17.39 seconds to load)
2 examples, 2 failures
```

Let's make these tests pass by updating our User model (app/models/user.rb) to look like this:

```
class User < ApplicationRecord
  validates_presence_of :first_name, :last_name
end
```

Now when we rerun the specs:

```
$ docker-compose exec web bin/rails spec
```

we can see that they pass:

```
..

Finished in 0.07523 seconds (files took 4.69 seconds to load)
2 examples, 0 failures
```

And that's all there is to it. Once set up, the key difference when using RSpec with Docker is simply that we have to prefix our commands with docker-compose exec web—hopefully, you're starting to get used to this.

Setting Up Rails System Tests

Rails system tests[3]—added in Rails 5.1[4]—allow you to perform high-level, end-to-end tests of your application. Rather than testing that individual functions or methods perform as they should (unit testing), they test the application based on how the user interacts with it—that is, via a web interface. They allow us to assert that when a user interacts with our application in a certain way (such as filling in forms, clicking links or buttons), the app responds as we'd expect (such as displaying the correct page, having the correct things appear on the page).

Although this kind of end-to-end test was possible previously—for example, with *RSpec Feature specs*[5]—system tests bring a number of benefits. We no longer have to worry about the cleanup of our database during the tests, which was commonly done using the Database Cleaner gem;[6] instead, system tests run the browser driver code in the same process as Rails, allowing the tests to be performed in transactions that are rolled back.

Though slower to run, end-to-end tests like these are arguably the most important type of tests for your app since they verify that the capabilities an app was created to provide actually work as expected. Even with 100 percent unit test coverage, one typo in a config file can stop the entire application from functioning correctly. The only way to know for sure is to load the app in a browser and actually use it. You can probably tell I'm a fan.

System specs rely on the Capybara gem[7] in order to function—this provides a nice domain-specific language (DSL) for interacting with the browser. Following the instructions for Capybara,[8] the first step is to install the gem.

---

3.   https://guides.rubyonrails.org/testing.html#system-testing

4.   https://guides.rubyonrails.org/5_1_release_notes.html#system-tests

5.   https://relishapp.com/rspec/rspec-rails/docs/feature-specs/feature-spec

6.   https://rubygems.org/gems/database_cleaner

7.   https://rubygems.org/gems/capybara

8.   https://github.com/teamcapybara/capybara#setup

Let's add it to our Gemfile now:

```
group :development, :test do
  # Call 'byebug' anywhere in the code to stop execution and get a debugger…
  gem 'byebug', platforms: [:mri, :mingw, :x64_mingw]
  gem 'rspec-rails', '~> 3.8'
  gem 'capybara', '~> 3.7'
end
```

Next we need to install this new gem by rebuilding the image. We'll recreate the web container at the same time:

```
$ docker-compose build web
$ docker-compose stop web
$ docker-compose up -d --force-recreate web
```

We're now ready to create our first system spec. By default, RSpec expects to find these in the spec/system directory, so let's create this now:

```
$ mkdir spec/system
```

Let's start by creating the file spec/system/page_views_spec.rb and edit it as follows:

```
require 'rails_helper'

RSpec.describe "PageViews" do
  it "shows the number of page views" do
    visit '/welcome'
    expect(page.text).to match(/This page has been viewed [0-9]+ times?!/)
  end
end
```

Linux Users: File Ownership

 Again, you will have to chown the files (see *File Ownership and Permissions*, on page 199):

```
$ sudo chown <your_user>:<your_group> -R .
```

Before we run this test, let's switch to using the RackTest driver for standard system tests. Not only is this faster, but it saves us having to install a full browser driver with JavaScript support (Selenium is the default) until we actually need it.

Edit spec/rails_helper.rb, adding the following lines just before the final end:

```
config.before(:each, type: :system) do
  driven_by :rack_test
end
```

This uses RSpec's before configuration hook to perform some of the setup before every system spec is run; specifically, we use the driven_by method—a new Rails method provided for system tests—to set the Capybara driver to rack_test.

With that done, let's run the tests:

```
$ docker-compose exec web rspec spec/system/
.

Finished in 27.2 seconds (files took 11.57 seconds to load)
1 example, 0 failures
```

Great! We've configured Capybara and our system specs.

Running Tests That Rely on JavaScript

OK, let's take this up a notch. Setting up testing with JavaScript support is not going to be so straightforward with Docker. But I think you're ready to handle it.

Imagine, if you will, that we have an enhanced version of our /welcome page that has extra behavior that only works with JavaScript enabled. In fact, when functioning correctly, this JavaScript literally adds the message "ENHANCED!" on the page.

Here's my rather crude implementation in app/views/welcome/index.html.erb:

```erb
<% content_for :head do %>
  <script type="text/javascript">
    document.addEventListener("DOMContentLoaded",function(){
      document.getElementsByTagName('h1')[0].append(' ENHANCED!');
    });
  </script>
<% end %>

<h1>This page has been viewed <%= pluralize(@page_hits, 'time') %>!</h1>
```

We also need a tweak to app/views/layouts/application.html.erb to make this work:

```erb
<!DOCTYPE html>
<html>
  <head>
    <title>Myapp</title>
    <%= csrf_meta_tags %>

    <%= stylesheet_link_tag 'application',
                            media: 'all',
                            'data-turbolinks-track': 'reload' %>

    <%= javascript_include_tag 'application',
                               'data-turbolinks-track': 'reload' %>
    <%= yield :head %>
  </head>
```

```
  <body>
    <%= yield %>
  </body>
</html>
```

Let's add a second scenario to our PageViews system spec to test this behavior (remember, our aim here is to demonstrate how to configure JavaScript testing, so I'll trust you to write more useful tests in your own apps):

```
Line 1  require 'rails_helper'

        RSpec.describe "PageViews" do
          it "shows the number of page views" do
     5      visit '/welcome'
            expect(page.text).to match(/This page has been viewed [0-9]+ times?!/)
          end

          it "is enhanced with JavaScript on", js: true do
    10      visit '/welcome'
            expect(page).to have_text("ENHANCED!")
          end
        end
```

As per the RSpec convention, we've indicated that this new scenario (line 9) is only expected to pass with JavaScript enabled, by specifying js: true.

However, we have a problem. As you may know, the default driver used by Capybara is RackTest, which, although fast to run, doesn't have JavaScript support. If we were to run the system specs now, they would fail even though (we believe) this feature is working.

To be able to run specs that rely on JavaScript being executed in the application, we have to use a different, more full-fledged driver. There are a number of options:

- Selenium,[9] which supports several browsers including Chrome with its recently announced headless Chrome support[10]

- Capybara-webkit,[11] a driver for the headless WebKit implementation from the Qt cross-platform toolkit

- Poltergeist,[12] a driver for headless WebKit using PhantomJS[13]

9. https://github.com/teamcapybara/capybara#selenium
10. https://developers.google.com/web/updates/2017/04/headless-chrome
11. https://github.com/thoughtbot/capybara-webkit
12. https://github.com/teampoltergeist/poltergeist
13. http://phantomjs.org

Rails system tests use Selenium by default, so we'll stick with that. I'm opting to go with Chrome via Selenium. Chrome is the most popular desktop browser, and people are saying good things about its headless support compared to Capybara-webkit.[14]

To use Selenium, we'll need to add the selenium-webdriver gem to our Gemfile:

```
group :development, :test do
  # Call 'byebug' anywhere in the code to stop execution and get a debugger…
  gem 'byebug', platforms: [:mri, :mingw, :x64_mingw]
  gem 'rspec-rails', '~> 3.8'
  gem 'capybara', '~> 3.7'
➤ gem 'selenium-webdriver', '~> 3.14'
end
```

and then install it by rebuilding our image and recreating our web container:

```
$ docker-compose build web
$ docker-compose stop web
$ docker-compose up -d --force-recreate web
```

But how are we going to run Chrome with Docker? The same way we typically run any software with Docker—in a container. There are prepared images for running standalone versions of Chrome, and in fact, we're going to use one such image maintained by Selenium itself.[15]

Let's add that to our Compose file:

```
selenium_chrome:
  image: selenium/standalone-chrome-debug
  logging:
    driver: none
  ports:
    - "5900:5900"
```

This adds a new service that we've chosen to call selenium_chrome, whose containers will be based on the selenium/standalone-chrome-debug image. We've opted for the debug,[16] rather than the standard version of this image,[17] because it includes and runs a VNC server. This gives us the option to visually see Chrome running inside the container using a VNC client—useful if you want to actually see the tests running.

We've also turned logging off by setting the logging driver to none because the Selenium Chrome image has noisy output that we don't need to see. We create

---

14. https://robots.thoughtbot.com/headless-feature-specs-with-chrome
15. https://hub.docker.com/r/selenium/standalone-chrome-debug/
16. https://hub.docker.com/r/selenium/standalone-chrome-debug/
17. https://hub.docker.com/r/selenium/standalone-chrome/

a port mapping so that the VNC server running inside the container on port 5900 is reachable from outside the container on that same port. You can check out Docker's docs for more details on the logging options available.[18]

Let's start our new service so Selenium Chrome is available for our system tests:

```
$ docker-compose up -d selenium_chrome
```

Problems Starting Chrome?

 If you get an error when starting the selenium_chrome service, it's likely because you have another VNC client running on port 5900. For example, on macOS, make sure you have Screen Sharing turned off in your System Preferences.

Next, we have to configure Capybara to use Chrome running in a container. Let's create the file spec/support/capybara.rb and add the following config:

```
Line 1  Capybara.register_driver :selenium_chrome_in_container do |app|
     2    Capybara::Selenium::Driver.new app,
     3      browser: :remote,
     4      url: "http://selenium_chrome:4444/wd/hub",
     5      desired_capabilities: :chrome
     6  end
```

This registers a new driver with Capybara—called :selenium_chrome_in_container—configured to use the Selenium driver to control a remote Selenium instance of Chrome running at http://selenium_chrome:4444/wd/hub (line 5.) Why this specific URL? Selenium listens for incoming client requests at http://<host>:<port>/wd/hub. Port 4444 is the default port that Selenium listens on, and the hostname selenium_chrome, which matches our new service in docker-compose.yml, will reach our container running Chrome. You may recall from Chapter 5, *Beyond the App: Adding Redis*, on page 59, that Compose sets up hostnames to reach other Compose services.

Linux Users: File Ownership

 As always, remember to chown the new file (see *File Ownership and Permissions*, on page 199):

```
$ sudo chown <your_user>:<your_group> -R .
```

Configuring RSpec System Tests

We've created a new Capybara driver, but how do we configure RSpec to use it?

First, we have to edit spec/rails_helper.rb to require our new Capybara driver so that it's loaded:

```
require 'rspec/rails'
# Add additional requires below this line. Rails is not loaded until this…
require_relative './support/capybara.rb'
```

Often apps will auto-require all .rb files inside the spec/support directory. If that's the case for your app, this require could be omitted.

OK, what next? Recall that earlier, we used RSpec's configuration hooks to set rack_test as the default driver for our system tests. We now need to make it so that non-JavaScript system tests continue to use that, whereas Java-Script tests (indicated with the js: true tag in the test definition) should use our new Selenium Chrome Capybara driver.

We can achieve this by adding the following lines to spec/rails_helper.rb (add them in between the previous before hook we added and the final end):

```
Line 1  config.before(:each, type: :system, js: true) do
  2      driven_by :selenium_chrome_in_container
  3      Capybara.server_host = "0.0.0.0"
  4      Capybara.server_port = 4000
  5      Capybara.app_host = 'http://web:4000'
  6    end
```

System specs that specify js: true will use this new config (ones without will continue to use our old config, which sets the rack_test driver). This new config sets the Capybara driver (line 2) to selenium_chrome_in_container: our new driver that runs the tests via our remote Selenium Chrome browser.

Since the browser executing the tests will be running in a separate container, rather than on the same machine, some additional config is required. Capybara will start a new Puma server to run a test version of our app. Normally, this just happens on localhost on the same machine that the tests are running on, and everything just works. Here, however, this test version of our app needs to be accessible *externally*, from the Selenium Chrome container. That means we have to start the test app on a known port—I've chosen port 4000 (line 4), but you could choose anything. Also, much like when we started the Rails server with the -b 0.0.0.0 to listen on all ports, Capybara must start the test app server listening on all IP addresses. That's why we set server_host to 0.0.0.0 (line 3); without this, the server would be started on localhost, and only incoming requests within the container would be serviced.

Finally, we need to tell Capybara to use a URL for the app that will work when connecting from within the Selenium Chrome container (line 5). Remember,

Docker sets up DNS entries to allow us to reference other services' containers by name. So the Selenium Chrome container would access the app running in our Rails container running the tests with the URL http://web:4000 (we previously configured the test server to start on port 4000).

Right. We're almost ready to try all this out, but first we must do one more thing. We've told Capybara to start the test app on port 4000, and we configured the tests that will be run remotely on our Selenium Chrome container to access this. However, currently port 4000 is not accessible from outside the web container, which currently only exposes port 3000.

Let's fix this by adding the following line to our web ports config in our docker-compose.yml:

```
ports:
  - "3000:3000"
  - "4000:4000"
```

To pick up this change, we need to stop our web container and --force-recreate it.

```
$ docker-compose stop web
Stopping myapp_web_1 ... done
$ docker-compose up -d --force-recreate web
Recreating myapp_web_1 ... done
```

Now we should be good to run the specs:

```
$ docker-compose exec web rspec spec/system/
.Capybara starting Puma...
* Version 3.12.0 , codename: Llamas in Pajamas
* Min threads: 0, max threads: 4
* Listening on tcp://0.0.0.0:4000
.

Finished in 31.17 seconds (files took 8.8 seconds to load)
2 examples, 0 failures
```

This time when we run the tests, our JavaScript-dependent system spec now passes.

Seeing the Tests Run

As I said before, we specifically chose the selenium/standalone-chrome-debug image because it includes a running VNC server. This allows us to connect and actually view tests as they run in the browser.

In order to see the desktop of our container, we'll need a VNC client to connect with. If you're on a Mac, you can use the Screen Sharing app that comes as standard on macOS. On Linux, it depends on your distribution and installed software, but installing a VNC client should be easy enough through your package manager. For Windows, there are several options,[19] some of which are free.

OK, VNC client at the ready? Go ahead and launch it and connect to vnc://localhost:5900. Port 5900 is the default port for VNC servers—you may remember that we exposed this port when we defined the selenium_chrome service in our docker-compose.yml. You should be prompted to enter a password, which is "secret".[20] Enter this now, and you should see a window open that looks something like:

This is showing us the Linux desktop that's running in our selenium_chrome service's container. If everything is working as we expect, when we rerun our tests, we should see something happen. Let's give it a whirl:

```
$ docker-compose exec web rspec spec/system/
```

In the VNC client window, you should see a new Chrome browser open up and load a page of our application (as shown in the figure on page 108.) The browser will close again very quickly, so you may want to add a sleep 10 in the middle of the JavaScript scenario to actually see the page once it's loaded.

19. https://www.techrepublic.com/blog/five-apps/five-apps-for-vnc-remote-desktop-access-on-windows/
20. https://github.com/SeleniumHQ/docker-selenium#debugging

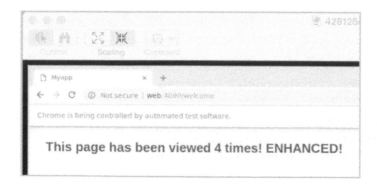

Headless Browsing

Being able to see our tests running is a useful option to have. We typically need it when something isn't working as expected and we want to see what's actually happening. However, most of the time we don't care about seeing the tests run—we just want them to run as fast as humanly (or is that computerly) possible. For that reason, we typically run our system specs in *headless* mode, without a browser window actually being displayed. Without the overhead of driving a real UI, the tests can run a lot faster.

To achieve this, let's register a second driver in spec/support/capybara.rb for running Selenium Chrome in headless mode:

```
require "selenium/webdriver"

Capybara.register_driver :selenium_chrome_in_container do |app|
  Capybara::Selenium::Driver.new app,
    browser: :remote,
    url: "http://selenium_chrome:4444/wd/hub",
    desired_capabilities: :chrome
end
```

```
Capybara.register_driver :headless_selenium_chrome_in_container do |app|
  Capybara::Selenium::Driver.new app,
    browser: :remote,
    url: "http://selenium_chrome:4444/wd/hub",
    desired_capabilities: Selenium::WebDriver::Remote::Capabilities.chrome(
      chromeOptions: { args: %w(headless disable-gpu) }
    )
end
```

The new Capybara driver definition is virtually identical to the first; the only difference is we specify the headless and disable-gpu when starting Chrome. Note that we also had to require selenium/webdriver since we need to use the Selenium::WebDriver::Remote::Capabilities class.

To switch to using this headless driver, we have to modify the RSpec config we added in spec/rails_helper.rb to use this driver for our JavaScript system specs:

```
config.before(:each, type: :system, js: true) do
  driven_by :headless_selenium_chrome_in_container

  Capybara.server_host = "0.0.0.0"
  Capybara.server_port = 4000
  Capybara.app_host = 'http://web:4000'
end
```

Now if you rerun the system specs:

```
$ docker-compose exec web rspec spec/system/
```

you won't actually see the browser appear in the VNC window, but the test will pass.

Debugging

No chapter on testing would be complete without some mention of how to debug our application when it isn't behaving as we'd expect.

Imagine there's a problem with our welcome_controller.rb. Let's use the byebug debugger that's included as standard with a Rails app. Let's add a byebug breakpoint to our welcome_controller.rb:

```
class WelcomeController < ApplicationController
  def index
    redis = Redis.new(host: "redis", port: 6379)
    redis.incr "page hits"

    @page_hits = redis.get "page hits"
    byebug
  end
end
```

Let's stop our Rails server:

```
$ docker-compose stop web
```

When we want an *interactive* session with a container, rather than using docker-compose up, we instead use docker-compose run. Let's start an interactive session with our web server like this:

```
$ docker-compose run --service-ports web
```

By default, docker-compose run will ignore the port mappings specified in our docker-compose.yml file for the service. The --service-ports option changes this behavior and ensures they are mapped; without this, our Rails server wouldn't be accessible on port 3000 from the browser.

Now, visit http://localhost:3000/welcome in the browser: the page will hang as the request hits our byebug breakpoint. Back in the terminal, you should see a familiar byebug interface waiting for you:

```
=> Booting Puma
=> Rails 5.2.2 application starting in development
=> Run `rails server -h` for more startup options
Puma starting in single mode...
«...»
[2, 11] in /usr/src/app/app/controllers/welcome_controller.rb
    2:   def index
    3:     redis = Redis.new(host: "redis", port: 6379)
    4:     redis.incr "page hits"
    5:
    6:     @page_hits = redis.get "page hits"
    7:     byebug
=>  8:   end
    9: end
   10:
   11:
(byebug)
```

Feel free to experiment here to verify it works; for example, you could output the @page_hits variable to see its value. When you're ready to exit, press c (for "continue"), then Enter; the request will continue as normal, and the page should display in the browser. Press Ctrl-C to stop the web container.

Before moving on, remember to remove the byebug breakpoint from welcome_controller.rb, then start up the web server again:

```
$ docker-compose up -d web
```

Rails Server Not Starting?

 If Rails fails to start because it thinks a server is already running, delete tmp/pids/server.pid on your local machine and try again. We'll see a better way to handle this in Chapter 9.

If you use IntelliJ or RubyMine, they have built-in support for using Ruby via docker-compose, including support for their debugger.[21]

Quick Recap

By now, using Docker should be starting to feel pretty familiar. In fact, much of this chapter was standard stuff we'd do in Rails—Docker got out of our way. Things got a little more tricky when it came to tests requiring JavaScript,

---

21. https://blog.jetbrains.com/ruby/2017/05/rubymine-2017-2-eap-1-docker-compose/

but having a ready-made image with Selenium-driven Chrome made the installation of these a breeze—that's where Docker shines.

In summary:

1. We set up and installed RSpec.

2. We saw how to run our specs in a Docker environment.

3. We set up system specs and ran tests using the default RackTest driver.

4. We got our system specs to work even when JavaScript is required, by configuring Capybara to use a Selenium-driven Chrome browser running in a separate container.

5. We made our JavaScript system tests faster by configuring headless Chrome in normal use.

6. We learned how to debug our application, even though it's running inside a container.

Although we've gradually been leveling up our Docker skills, you may have noticed one area where things have felt sluggish—rebuilding our image still feels slow whenever we need to add or modify our gems. In the next chapter, we'll see what we can do to mitigate this and speed up image builds.

## CHAPTER 9

Advanced Gem Management

We now have a working development environment, all based on Docker. However, there's one area that is worth a bit more thought: gem management.

Up until now, to install or update gems, we've simply been rebuilding the image for our Rails app. This works because bundle install is one of the steps in our Dockerfile. However, as we'll see in a moment, there's a slight downside to this approach compared to what we're used to when managing gems in a non-Dockerized environment (you may have already spotted this).

In this chapter, we'll explore an alternative approach to managing our gems that attempts to avoid the drawback by making different trade-offs (it's more complicated for a start).

Whether you stick with the simple approach we've been using so far, or this new approach, is completely up to you. I will present the technique, explain the trade-offs, and then you can choose based on your needs and preferences. Deal?

The Downside to Our Existing Approach

Our current approach for managing gems is to rebuild the image any time we need to update our gems. However, you may have noticed that any time we change our Gemfile, even if it's just adding a single gem, *all* our gems have to be reinstalled from scratch. As a result, updating our gems takes longer than we're typically used to.

Why does this happen?

Bundler and Docker images are both trying to achieve the same goal of ensuring a consistent environment, but they achieve it in different ways. Docker's image-build process breaks some of Bundler's key assumptions, which means it doesn't quite work how we're used to.

Bundler was primarily designed for use on a long-running system where installed gems hang around; the main use case is updating the set of *currently installed* gems. However, rebuilding an image is akin to building a new machine from scratch—in this scenario, Bundler is *not* being used on a long-running system. This, in essence, is the source of the issue.

Let's have another look at our Dockerfile and walk through what happens when we rebuild our image. Here are the last seven lines:

```
Line 1  COPY Gemfile* /usr/src/app/
     2  WORKDIR /usr/src/app
     3  RUN bundle install
     4
     5  COPY . /usr/src/app/
     6
     7  CMD ["bin/rails", "s", "-b", "0.0.0.0"]
```

When we modify our Gemfile, it busts the cache for line 1 of the extract. That means the cached intermediate layers for subsequent steps are thrown away, including the gems previously installed in the bundle install step (line 3). When the image build reaches this step again, it's as if we've never run bundle install on this machine before. No wonder the gems must be reinstalled from scratch.

How big a problem is this?

It depends on your situation. You may have more or less gems in your project(s), and more or less tolerance for waiting while gems install. The thing our basic approach has going for it is just that—it's basic. No extra things to configure or remember—just rebuild your image and you're done. This may be a perfectly acceptable option for many people.

However, if the time waiting for gems to build bothers you, then it's worth considering another option.

Using a Gem Cache Volume

As we've seen, the key problem is that Docker's image building, akin to building a machine from scratch, is at odds with the caching of gems with Bundler. What if, instead of fighting the image build process, we bypassed it? We've already seen on page 81 how volumes provide persistent file storage that's separate from the container filesystem; we can use this to solve our thorny problem.

Here's the gist.

By mounting a volume in the directory where Bundler installs our gems, we can execute Bundler commands to populate and manage the gems on this volume, which effectively becomes a local gem cache. Remember that a mounted volume overlays, and is separate from, the container's filesystem; its files persist beyond the life cycle of the container itself.

Let's see how this works in practice.

First, we need to configure Bundler to use an explicit, known directory for installing gems to.../gems, say. We do this by setting the BUNDLE_PATH environment variable. Let's update our Dockerfile as follows:

```
COPY Gemfile* /usr/src/app/
WORKDIR /usr/src/app
```
➤ `ENV BUNDLE_PATH /gems`

```
RUN bundle install

COPY . /usr/src/app/

CMD ["bin/rails", "s", "-b", "0.0.0.0"]
```

The real magic, though, comes in our docker-compose.yml file:

```
version: '3'

services:
  web:
    build: .
    ports:
      - "3000:3000"
      - "4000:4000"
    volumes:
      - .:/usr/src/app
➤      - gem_cache:/gems
    env_file:
      - .env/development/web
      - .env/development/database
    environment:
      - WEBPACKER_DEV_SERVER_HOST=webpack_dev_server

  webpack_dev_server:
    build: .
    command: ./bin/webpack-dev-server
    ports:
      - 3035:3035
    volumes:
      - .:/usr/src/app
➤      - gem_cache:/gems
    env_file:
      - .env/development/web
      - .env/development/database
    environment:
      - WEBPACKER_DEV_SERVER_HOST=0.0.0.0
```

```
  redis:
    image: redis
  database:
    image: postgres
    env_file:
      - .env/development/database
    volumes:
      - db_data:/var/lib/postgresql/data
  selenium_chrome:
    image: selenium/standalone-chrome-debug
    logging:
      driver: none
    ports:
      - "5900:5900"
volumes:
  db_data:
➤ gem_cache:
```

Just like we did in *Decoupling Data from the Container*, on page 81, we create a new named volume—this time called gem_cache—by adding this to our list of volumes. Compose will handle the details of where this volume is stored.

Then, in the definition for our web service, we tell Compose to mount our gem_cache volume at /gems in the container, which is now where Bundler is configured to install gems to.

To try out this approach, we first need to rebuild our image:

```
$ docker-compose build web
```

Our web service should already be stopped, and we removed its container earlier, so to create a new web container along with the gem_cache volume, we just do:

```
$ docker-compose up -d web
Creating volume "myapp_gem_cache" with default driver
Recreating myapp_web_1 ... done
```

With the app running, and our gem_cache created, we can now execute Bundler commands directly against our running web container:

```
$ docker-compose exec web bundle install
```

Thanks to our BUNDLE_PATH, this installs the projects' gems to the container's /gems directory. As we know, that's where our gem_cache volume is mounted, courtesy of our volume mapping. As a consequence, all our gems are now installed on our gem_cache volume.

With our gem cache populated, let's try installing a new gem. Imagine we want to add Devise for authentication. Let's add it to our Gemfile:

```
...
gem 'redis', '~> 4.0'
# Authentication
gem 'devise', '~> 4.4', '>= 4.4.1'
...
```

OK. Now, like we'd typically do in a non-Dockerized environment, we install the gem by running the bundle install command:

```
$ docker-compose exec web bundle install
```

You should see output similar to the following:

```
The dependency tzinfo-data (>= 0) will be unused by any of the platforms
Bundler is installing for. Bundler is installing for ruby but the dependency
is only for x86-mingw32, x86-mswin32, x64-mingw32, java. To add those plat-
forms to the bundle, run `bundle lock --add-platform x86-mingw32 x86-mswin32
x64-mingw32 java`.
Fetching gem metadata from https://rubygems.org/.........
Fetching gem metadata from https://rubygems.org/.
Resolving dependencies.....
Using rake 12.3.2
Using concurrent-ruby 1.1.4
«...»
Fetching warden 1.2.8
Installing warden 1.2.8
Fetching devise 4.5.0
Installing devise 4.5.0
«...»
Using turbolinks-source 5.2.0
Using turbolinks 5.2.0
Using uglifier 4.1.20
Using web-console 3.7.0
Using webpacker 3.5.5
Bundle complete! 21 Gemfile dependencies, 90 gems now installed.
Bundled gems are installed into `/gems`
```

The output shows that Devise is the only gem that's installed—the others are reused from our gem cache.

There's one final complication: our webpack_dev_server service. Since this uses the same Dockerfile as our web service, we also need to rebuild its image:

```
$ docker-compose build webpack_dev_server
```

Similarly, we then need to recreate the webpack_dev_server container from the new image:

```
$ docker-compose up -d webpack_dev_server
Recreating myapp_webpack_dev_server_1 ... done
```

Since we're using the same `gem_cache` volume for both our `web` and `webpack_dev_server` services, gems added by updating the `web` service will automatically be available to the `webpack_dev_server` service, and vice versa.

Let's review the benefits and downsides to this strategy:

Pros:

- Speeds up gem management for all Bundler actions: adding, removing, or updating gems

- Uses familiar `bundle install` workflow predominantly during development

Cons:

- Bundle commands only update our local volume; we still ultimately need to build the image

- Possibility for confusion over which gems are being loaded or used

- Extra complexity of changes to both `Dockerfile` and `docker-compose.yml`, plus the need to understand the nuance of gems being overlaid in local volume

Many Rails developers will find this approach appealing because we explicitly manage our gems with Bundler like we're used to, instead of relying on rebuilding our image to run `bundle install`. If you can get your head around the complexity, this strategy will definitely make your local development feel snappier, especially if you're making a lot of gem changes.

Quick Recap

Who knew that gem management could be such a hot topic? With this new option at your disposal, you should feel ready for anything.

Let's take a look back at what we covered in this chapter:

1. We discussed the downsides to our previous approach to managing gems: any gem changes required all gems to be reinstalled from scratch.

2. We explored a way to speed up gem changes that involved creating a volume for caching our gems. By mounting the volume into our container (and setting `BUNDLE_PATH`), we could manage our gems manually and benefit from faster builds.

Hopefully, you're also starting to appreciate the meta point here: how problems with our Docker setup can be identified, thought through, and eventually solved in creative ways. The more you use Docker and understand how it works, the more you'll start spotting opportunities for improvements yourself.

Good as it is, Compose is not without failings. Before we close out the development section, in the spirit of full disclosure, we're going to explore a couple of common pain points you may encounter when using Compose. In the following chapter, you'll learn about these irritations and what we can do to minimize their impact.

## CHAPTER 10

Some Minor Irritations

Well, isn't this embarrassing.

Unfortunately, Compose has a couple of irritating issues. Since you may have encountered them in the preceding chapters, or as you go on to use Compose yourself, it seems irresponsible to ignore them. Here we'll take a quick look at each in turn.

Fortunately, we can work around the first issue—with a little effort. However, the second problem remains elusively unsolved.

Rails tmp/pids/server.pid Not Cleaned Up

For some reason, occasionally upon terminating the app with Compose (pressing `Ctrl-C`), the Rails server doesn't seem to shut down cleanly, and its server.pid file—which Rails stores in tmp/pids/—isn't deleted. This means that upon starting the app again with:

```
$ docker-compose up
```

you may find yourself confronted by the following error in the output:

```
...
A server is already running. Check /usr/src/app/tmp/pids/server.pid
...
```

The existence of the pid file makes the Rails server starting up believe that there's a server already running, so it won't launch.

Rails saves the server.pid file in tmp/pids. Since we're mounting our local app directory into the container, the file ends up in the tmp/pids/ directory *on our local machine* and is persisted until we delete it.

How do we solve this?

Since we're mounting our app directory into the container, it's easy enough to delete the server.pid file manually:

```
$ rm tmp/pids/server.pid
```

This done, the Rails server should now start:

```
$ docker-compose up
```

You should see in the output that Rails is now up and running. However, this doesn't really solve the problem if it keeps happening. Luckily, we can put in place a workaround.

Let's see the workaround, and then discuss it:

1. Create a docker-entrypoint.sh file in your Rails root as follows:

   ```
   #!/bin/sh
   set -e

   if [ -f tmp/pids/server.pid ]; then
     rm tmp/pids/server.pid
   fi

   exec "$@"
   ```

2. Make this file executable:

   ```
   $ chmod +x docker-entrypoint.sh
   ```

3. Specify an ENTRYPOINT instruction in our Dockerfile file by adding the following line just before the final CMD instruction:

   ```
   ENTRYPOINT ["./docker-entrypoint.sh"]
   ```

4. Stop, rebuild, and restart the web service:

   ```
   $ docker-compose stop web
   $ docker-compose build web
   $ docker-compose up -d web
   ```

So what's all this doing?

An entrypoint is *prepended* to the command run upon starting a new container. In our case, we've set ./docker-entrypoint.sh as the ENTRYPOINT for the web service. This means, when we start a new web container, rather than simply running the default command of:

```
bin/rails s -b 0.0.0.0
```

it will actually run this, thanks to our new ENTRYPOINT instruction:

```
./docker-entrypoint.sh bin/rails s -b 0.0.0.0
```

Since this shell script will be run, we need to give the file execute permissions, as we do in step 2.

What is our docker-entrypoint.sh shell script actually doing? In case you're not familiar with Bash, let's quickly go through it step by step (feel free to skip ahead if it's already clear).

```
Line 1  #!/bin/sh
     2  set -e
     3
     4  if [ -f tmp/pids/server.pid ]; then
     5    rm tmp/pids/server.pid
     6  fi
     7
     8  exec "$@"
```

It's good practice in Bash scripts to start with set -e (line 2)—this makes the script fail fast if any subsequent commands terminate with an error (non-zero exit status).

The if statement on line 4 checks to see if the tmp/pids/server.pid file exists; if it does, we delete it on line 5. This is the cleanup portion of the script that ensures our Rails server will always start, even if the server.pid file is left behind.

However, ultimately we want the container to start our Rails server, not this Bash script. That's where the exec command on line 8 comes in. It says, "Replace the currently running process (this Bash script) by running the following program"—almost as if the shell script had never existed. But what program does exec run? The "$@" means "all arguments that were provided to this Bash script," which in our case would be bin/rails s -b 0.0.0.0. So effectively, we're saying, "Replace this running Bash script with a Rails server."

In summary, docker-entrypoint.sh acts as a wrapper script, giving us an opportunity to do our small cleanup of the pid file and then start up the Rails server as if nothing had happened. Now you can just run docker-compose up to your heart's content, safe in the knowledge that this pesky bug won't affect you.

Entrypoints, especially following this pattern, are a good tool to have in your arsenal; you may find other, creative uses for them. It's also worth knowing that you can specify an entrypoint directly in the Dockerfile too, using the ENTRYPOINT instruction. See Docker's docs for more details.[1]

---

1. https://docs.docker.com/engine/reference/builder/#entrypoint

Compose Intermittently Aborts with Ctrl-C

When you start your application with Compose in the default, *attached* mode—in other words, *without* the -d option—Compose connects to each container's stdout, tailing the output.

When you press Ctrl-C, Compose is supposed to instruct the containers to terminate by sending the main process the SIGTERM signal. The process should exit gracefully and then the container should terminate. When this happens correctly, the Compose output on pressing Ctrl-C is:

```
Killing myapp_web_1 ... done
Gracefully stopping... (press Ctrl+C again to force)
```

However, maybe 10–50 percent of the time for me, instead of the containers shutting down gracefully, we get this:

```
^CERROR: Aborting.
```

and the termination fails, leaving the containers still running. Not good.

Unfortunately, this seems to be a long-standing,[2] known[3] issue.[4] It seems to be caused by a problem in PyInstaller, an open source tool for creating executables from Python scripts, which Compose relies on.

The issue is an irritation rather than a showstopper. We can manually shut down the containers by issuing a docker-compose stop (or kill) command. However, although it seems to be an issue with a third-party dependency, it can't help but undermine our feeling of confidence in Compose itself, which is a shame.

Despite researching the issue and attempting the various, suggested fixes, I've been unable to find a workaround to prevent it. If you find yourself affected, my advice is simply to avoid starting your application in attached mode, and instead, always use *detached* mode with the -d option. To date, I haven't experienced the issue with that.

Quick Recap

No software is perfect, but it's unfortunate when your experience with using a tool is diminished due to bugs. I have to confess: it pained me to write this chapter. I wanted your experience of using Docker to be uniformly positive.

---

2. https://github.com/docker/compose/issues/2904
3. https://github.com/docker/compose/issues/3317
4. https://github.com/docker/compose/issues/3347

In the end, though, I felt these issues were important enough to bring to your attention. Hopefully, you should now be aware of the main problems and prepared to face them.

Let's review what we covered in this chapter:

1. We explored an issue where Rails' tmp/pids/server.pid file doesn't always get removed upon terminating the containers.

2. We learned about *entrypoints*, which are prepended to the command run on starting a new container.

3. We utilized an entrypoint to create a wrapper script that deletes the tmp/pids/server.pid on starting a container, working around the issue.

4. We discussed an issue where Compose intermittently aborts instead of terminating containers gracefully, deciding that the best approach to avoid it may be running Compose in detached mode (-d.)

OK, enough about annoyances. It's time to think about the positives.

Closing Thoughts on Docker in Development

As we draw to the close of this section on development, let's take a moment to reflect on what we've achieved. At first glance, it's easy to mistakenly think we've gone through a fair amount of effort only to arrive back where we started—with a standard, working Rails app.

In fact, though, we've achieved some major benefits:

*   Our Dockerfile and docker-compose.yml file give us a declarative description of our entire application—with all its required parts, such the database—helping to give a clear picture of what makes up the application.

*   We can spin up the entire application with a single command—even with nothing previously installed. Docker downloads and installs what we need.

*   We've eliminated the need to manually install our app's main software dependencies on our local machine. No more fiddling with getting Redis, Postgres, or even Ruby installed and running on compatible versions across the whole team. Docker is taking care of all of this for us.

*   That last point is a big one. It also means that our app can run on any machine with Docker installed. It gives us freedom and portability.

*   Upgrading parts of our application is as simple as updating the version number of the image we refer to in our Compose file. It's a breeze to see how our app works on a newer version of Ruby, for example.

For all these reasons, using Docker in development is useful in and of itself—you should feel proud for having reached this milestone. However, the journey doesn't stop here. Docker can bring even more benefits, as we prepare to move toward production.

Part II

Toward Production

Now that we've got the basics down of how to develop our app with Docker, we've got bigger fish to fry. In this section, we'll take our Dockerized Rails app and really start going places.

How do we get our application into the eager hands of users? That's the key question we'll be answering as we explore the real-world considerations along the way.

Buckle up, because where we're going, we don't need roads.

CHAPTER 11

The Production Landscape

Docker, and more generally, containerization establishes a new paradigm for packaging, running, and coordinating pieces of software. It's no surprise that this has a major impact on the way we deliver and manage software running in production. If you're inexperienced with operations, particularly now that Docker is in the mix, this world can feel like a maze. So, before we get our hands dirty with preparing to deploy our app in a production-like environment, we first need to familiarize ourselves with the lay of the land.

In this chapter, we'll start with a refresher on what it means to deliver and run software in production. Next, we'll explore how Docker shifts that landscape, and what delivery looks like if you embrace Docker. We'll cover the various hosting options, the tools you'll encounter (and their purpose), and the trade-offs you'll need to consider when choosing what you'll use for your production environment.

This chapter is unique in that it's purely informational: there are no practical steps to follow along with. So put your feet up, relax for a moment, and enjoy the change of pace.

The "Ops" in DevOps

Our focus as software developers is often on the development phase, with its discovery, analysis, testing, and building activities.

Depending on your work environment, you may or may not be heavily involved in operations—or just *Ops*—which involves delivering and running software in production. We can break this down into a number of different areas:

1. Provisioning

2. Configuration management

3. Release management

4. Monitoring and alerting

5. Operating

Although you probably have some idea of what these things mean, let's describe them so that we're on the same page.

Provisioning—also known as creating stuff. Software needs computers and resources to run on. Ensuring there are enough computing resources available—and creating them if not—is an important part of that. In fact, it's not just *machines* or *instances* that we need; when deploying apps to the cloud, we may also need other physical or virtual infrastructure, such as:

- Networks, also known as virtual private clouds (VPCs)
- Network address translation (NAT) gateways
- Routers
- Firewalls
- Internet gateways
- Proxies
- Security rules

Configuration management. Once our raw infrastructure has been created, it typically isn't ready to perform its true purpose in life; it has to be configured. For some (possibly virtual) infrastructure, such as routers or firewalls, this means ensuring they have the right settings or rules applied. For a server, it typically means installing the necessary software packages and dependencies needed to run an application.

Release management. Most systems need regular maintenance or continued development, which implies an ongoing need to deploy—or *release*—newer versions. Typically, we'd like to be able to release easily, repeatedly at any time, and with minimal or no impact to users of the system. This can be achieved through automation, good tooling, and techniques such as *blue-green deploys* or *canary releases*. Additionally, when things go wrong, the ability to roll back to a known-good version of the software can be invaluable.

Monitoring and alerting. In a perfect world, our application, once deployed, would perform as expected forever. In reality, things go wrong: servers fail, software has bugs, our assumptions don't hold true. Rather than bury our heads in the sand, we proactively take steps to know the health of our software and how well it's functioning. This typically involves tracking health metrics for the system and being alerted when things start to go wrong.

Operating. In the day-to-day running of production systems, there are some common things we may need to do: scaling up to handle increased load, scaling down to save costs, diagnosing and debugging issues, and generally, keeping the lights on. Smart operations teams try to automate as much as possible to minimize human error and free up their time so they can be proactive rather than fighting fires.

Adopting Docker changes the way we think about many of these areas.

Take configuration management, for example. Although tools like Chef, Puppet, or Ansible are extremely popular, their role in a containerized world is considerably diminished. With Docker, each piece of software has its dependencies baked into its image, isolating it from those in another container. This dramatically simplifies the problem. Since app-level dependencies are managed by the app itself, in its Dockerfile, configuring your infrastructure instances is largely just a case of ensuring that Docker is installed.

As we'll see shortly, Docker also has other implications, especially on how we release and operate our software.

Container Orchestration

Docker has changed the Ops landscape in two key ways. Firstly, its built-in delivery mechanism—the ability to *push* images to a Docker Registry and *pull* them down as needed—solves a common question: how do I get my software onto the target machine? Secondly, containers let us treat hugely disparate software in essentially the same way; we use the same mechanism to start, stop, and restart containers, whatever they happen to be running.

This standardization, both in terms of delivery mechanism and how we manage software, reshapes the way we think of operations. The focus shifts to how we configure, run, and update the multiple containers that make up an application *in concert*, a process known as (container) *orchestration*.

A new breed of tools has emerged to help orchestrate our app containers; they're named (rather uncreatively) *orchestrators*.

So what do these orchestrators do for us? First, they provide an environment or *platform* on which we can run and manage our containerized applications. They do this by creating an abstraction above the (physical or virtual) servers needed to run the software. When deploying applications, it's more convenient to think of our group of "compute" servers as a single logical unit: a cluster. This lets us say things like, "Let's deploy this app to the cluster," without caring how it gets deployed or on exactly which instance—we can (mostly) let our orchestration layer handle those details for us.

Since orchestrators provide the platform for running our apps, they are central to releasing new software (release management), knowing and managing how our cluster is using its resources (configuration management), and tasks like restarting services or scaling to match demand (operating).

What's nice about these tools is that they're declarative rather than imperative. Instead of our having to give the orchestrator a list of instructions that, if it follows, will achieve our desired state, we simply specify the desired state, and the orchestrator figures out how to achieve and maintain it. This allows us to think at a higher level, with the orchestrator handling many of the uninteresting, low-level details for us.

Because orchestrators understand the desired state, they are able to be smarter and more resilient to failure. If the code running in one of the containers crashes for some reason, the orchestrator can automatically restart it. If an entire node in the cluster fails, meaning all the containers it had been running are gone, again the orchestrator can recover and start up new replacement containers on the remaining nodes.

When you want to release a new version of your software, you tell the orchestrator that the desired state now uses your newer version of an image, and the orchestrator gets to work updating it. Orchestrators therefore play a key role in deployment and provide capabilities to perform rolling updates to help achieve zero-downtime deploys.

Orchestrators can help in other ways, too. Providing keys and sensitive configuration to apps is an age-old problem. However, in order to function, orchestrators need a secure, distributed way of managing the internal state of the cluster and communicating parts of it to nodes and containers on a need-to-know basis. That sounds suspiciously similar to distributed secret management. It's no surprise then that orchestrators expose secret management as an application-level feature.

Finally, as orchestrators play such a critical role at the heart of your production environment, they tend to have highly sophisticated security features—such as automatic key rotation—built in.

A Tale of Two Orchestrators: Swarm and Kubernetes

There are currently two competing orchestration layers that can be used with Docker: Swarm and Kubernetes. Both have many similarities but also significant differences.

Swarm (or Swarm *mode*)—Docker's homegrown solution—has been built into the Docker Engine since version 1.12, so you already have it installed. Although it took some time to become production-ready, Swarm is now a mature, capable, low-ceremony orchestrator. While it's still missing one or two desirable features (such as autoscaling), it's a well-thought-out piece of software and puts a lot of power at your fingertips. You'll get to experience Swarm first-hand in the upcoming chapters.

The other big player is Kubernetes, which is an open source tool created by Google, but it is now under the care of the Cloud Native Computing Foundation (CNCF).[1] Not only does Kubernetes support autoscaling, but it also provides more control over how your apps are architected. However, this rich feature set and expressiveness comes at a cost: it is considerably more complex than Swarm, takes more effort to learn, and its config files are more verbose. Additionally, installing Kubernetes by hand can be a lengthy and complicated task itself.

Kubernetes and Swarm have a similar high-level architecture. Both distinguish between worker nodes that run containers and manager nodes that manage the workers and orchestrate containers on them. One notable difference is that Swarm manager nodes can run workload containers *in addition* to their cluster management and orchestration role, whereas Kubernetes manager nodes can't. Also of note, Kubernetes currently uses offensive master/slave terminology to refer to manager and worker nodes, though I am hopeful this will soon be changed.[2]

When learning either Swarm or Kubernetes, getting to grips with their conceptual models[3,4] is key. Although there are similarities, each requires some getting used to. For example, Swarm has the concept of a stack, which envisions the application as a group of underlying services. Kubernetes, on the other hand, breaks this down further into a Deployment, made up of ReplicaSets, which in turn are made up of Pods.

---

1. https://www.cncf.io
2. https://github.com/kubernetes/website/issues/6525
3. https://docs.docker.com/engine/swarm/key-concepts/
4. https://kubernetes.io/docs/concepts/

Here's a very high-level summary of the two:

	Swarm	Kubernetes
Open source	Yes	Yes
Created by	Docker	Google
Overseen by	Docker	CNCF
Installation	Simple	Complex
Learning curve	Easy	Difficult
Feature set	Smaller	Large
Built-in autoscaling?	No	Yes
Community support	Good	Excellent

Although Swarm still has its place, Kubernetes seems to have gained a lot of traction and mindshare, and is fast becoming the de facto standard for orchestration. In fact, in a nod to this, Docker has added built-in Kubernetes support out of the box.[5] In reality, Swarm vs. Kubernetes is not an either or: it's worth spending some time to become familiar with both and having both options available to you.

With that in mind, Swarm is going to be our focus in the remaining chapters. It has a simpler conceptual model and more succinct config, making it a better learning tool. Picking up Kubernetes will be easier having experienced Swarm, since you'll have a good feel for how orchestrators work.

One final point: although Swarm and Kubernetes are the two main orchestrators, some hosting providers have their own, platform-specific orchestration layer—notably, Amazon Elastic Container Service (Amazon ECS).

IaaS vs. CaaS

Now that we have a better understanding of where container orchestrators fit in, there's still a choice to be made if you're considering deploying containers to the cloud. You can either manage things at the infrastructure level and set up the orchestrator yourself, or you can use a container platform that handles the underlying infrastructure and provides a preinstalled orchestrator ready for you to deploy and scale your containers.

The former—known as Infrastructure as a Service (IaaS) platforms—are bare-bones offerings. They give you all the low-level building blocks to create the environment for your applications to run. As you would expect, this gives you the most flexibility and customization in terms of tailoring your environment

---

5. https://www.docker.com/products/orchestration

for your own needs. However, you have to do the work of provisioning your instances, configuring them, and installing your orchestration layer.

The latter—known as Containers as a Service (CaaS) platforms—are the closest thing to Heroku in a containerized world. They let you focus on your app and worry less about the infrastructure it runs on. For many, this is a popular option to get started. It's fast to get something up and running, and you offload a lot of the responsibilities, including many security considerations, to the platform. However, this comes at the price of less flexibility and customization—you're limited by the capabilities exposed by the platform.

The choice is not as discrete as it sounds. Even across different CaaS platforms, you'll find that more or less work is done for you.

Next, we'll look at some options around tools for provisioning IaaS infrastructure, were you to go down that route, before taking a brief tour of the big players in the CaaS space.

Provisioning Your Infrastructure

If you go down the IaaS route, in theory you can go with any cloud provider; they are just providing the raw infrastructure that you'll run your Docker containers on top of.

Here are some of the big players that you've probably heard of:

- Amazon AWS[6]
- Microsoft Azure[7]
- Google Compute Engine (GCE)[8]
- DigitalOcean[9]

However, you're going to need to provision your infrastructure, and in particular, the instances that Docker and your orchestration layer will be installed on. There are a number of tools that can assist you in this endeavor.

Docker Machine

Docker Machine[10] is a standalone tool for provisioning and managing Docker-ready instances. It not only creates an instance, but it installs Docker on the

---

6. httpsi//aws.amazon.com
7. https://azure.microsoft.com
8. https://cloud.google.com/compute/
9. https://www.digitalocean.com
10. https://docs.docker.com/machine/overview/

instance at the same time. This makes Docker Machine a really lightweight, friendly tool to get started with.

Docker Machine uses the adapter pattern,[11] providing different *drivers* capable of creating instances on a wide variety of platforms.[12] We'll use this shortly to create local VirtualBox instances on page 155 and then create cloud-based infrastructure on page 173.

Sometimes you need to provision more than just instances. Perhaps you may have security constraints that need to be enforced, or maybe specific networking requirements that involve the creation of networking devices (firewalls, NAT gateways, and so on) in a specific arrangement. In this case, Docker Machine alone wouldn't be enough; you'd have to consider other tools to assist.

Chef, Puppet, and Ansible

Traditionally, configuration management tools like Chef, Ansible, and Puppet have been used to provision infrastructure and configure it, including installing and managing software on instances. However, as we've already discussed, since Docker images are now responsible for most of your server configuration, the need for these other tools is greatly diminished.

Additionally, these tools all predate Docker—especially Puppet (2005) and Chef (2009)—so they weren't born out of a worldview that included containers. That said, they can still be used to bootstrap a cluster with Docker and your orchestration layer, but depending on your needs, may be overkill.

Terraform

Released in 2014, a year *after* Docker, HashiCorp's Terraform is the relative newcomer to the scene. Rather than being a fully fledged configuration management system, it considers itself an *infrastructure orchestrator*, with the more modest aim of provisioning and updating your infrastructure in a safe, controlled way.

It has only lightweight capabilities for configuring servers, allowing you to use other tools for this where it makes sense.[13] However, because only minimal server configuration is needed when using Docker, going Terraform-only is a lightweight and popular choice.[14]

---

11. https://en.wikipedia.org/wiki/Adapter_pattern
12. https://docs.docker.com/machine/drivers/
13. https://www.terraform.io/intro/vs/chef-puppet.html
14. https://blog.gruntwork.io/why-we-use-terraform-and-not-chef-puppet-ansible-saltstack-or-cloudformation-7989dad2865c

CaaS Platforms

Now that we've had a brief overview of our options if we choose to build on top of IaaS, let's turn our attention to the Container as a Service (CaaS) space.

As we've already discussed, CaaS offerings let you hit the ground running faster. They provide a managed service, where your starting point is a platform capable of running Dockerized applications.

In this area, *Kubernetes is king.* It is the predominant orchestration service offered by providers. This means that, once your Kubernetes workload cluster is up and running, you interact with it via the kubectl command to deploy, update, or scale your app. Similarly, your config manifests that describe the services you want running and how they should be connected will need to be in Kubernetes format.

Each offering is at a slightly different place in terms of features and maturity, so let's review the major players.

Amazon Elastic Container Service

The odd one out in this list, Amazon Elastic Container Service (Amazon ECS),[15] sports Amazon's own container orchestration layer, rather than Kubernetes.

The AWS *way*—ECS being no exception—is to provide the building blocks to architect your cloud infrastructure and apps from the ground up. This gives you very fine-grained control, but the trade-off is that you are exposed to additional complexity and have more work to hook things together. Most people either love it or hate it.

The service can be managed through the AWS Management Console[16] or via the ECS CLI,[17] both of which let you provision the infrastructure needed. Additionally, CloudFormation[18]—Amazon's proprietary infrastructure provisioning language—can also be used.

In ECS, you describe your application's containers using config files known as task definitions[19] in JSON format. It also provides compatibility with

---

15. https://aws.amazon.com/ecs/
16. https://aws.amazon.com/console/
17. https://docs.aws.amazon.com/AmazonECS/latest/developerguide/ECS_CLI.html
18. https://aws.amazon.com/cloudformation/
19. https://docs.aws.amazon.com/AmazonECS/latest/developerguide/task_definitions.html

Compose files[20]—with some caveats—which can let you sidestep the native task definition format.

Despite this compatibility with Compose, there's no getting around the need to understand ECS's conceptual model, which includes the heady delights of ECS clusters, services, tasks, Application Load Balancers (ALBs) and Elastic Load Balancers (ELBs), VPCs, and more.

Google Kubernetes Engine

Google Kubernetes Engine (GKE)[21] offers a true CaaS model that lets you forget about the underlying hardware. It provides fully managed clusters, meaning that they look after the running of the infrastructure and ensure clusters remain healthy.

Creating a basic cluster is done with a short, clear command—for example:

```
$ gcloud container clusters create guestbook --num-nodes=3
```

This says, "Create new cluster called guestbook with three nodes" and, as you'd expect, GKE handles the creation of the infrastructure for you. There are lots of other possible cluster configurations,[22] such as multiregion clusters.

GKE seems to be the most mature, user-friendly offering in the space—not entirely surprising given that Kubernetes was created at Google.

Amazon Elastic Container Service for Kubernetes

A key drawback of Amazon Elastic Container Service for Kubernetes (Amazon EKS)[23] at the time of writing is its limited availability—currently only in US North Virginia (us-east-1), US Oregon (us-west-2), and US Ohio (us-east-2) regions.[24] However, this will no doubt improve over time.

Unlike GKE, the underlying AWS underpinnings leak through. For example, since EKS needs the ability to create Amazon Elastic Compute Cloud (Amazon EC2)[25] instances on your behalf, you have to create an AWS Identify & Access Management (IAM)[26] service role with the correct permissions in order to get started with EKS.[27]

---

20. https://docs.aws.amazon.com/AmazonECS/latest/developerguide/cmd-ecs-cli-compose.html
21. https://cloud.google.com/kubernetes-engine/
22. https://cloud.google.com/kubernetes-engine/docs/how-to/creating-a-cluster
23. https://aws.amazon.com/eks/
24. https://aws.amazon.com/about-aws/global-infrastructure/regional-product-services/
25. https://aws.amazon.com/ec2/
26. https://aws.amazon.com/iam/
27. https://docs.aws.amazon.com/eks/latest/userguide/getting-started.html

This is evident in the command to create a cluster:

```
$ aws eks create-cluster
  --name prod \
  --role-arn \
    arn:aws:iam::012345678910:role/eks-service-role-AWSServiceRoleFor... \
  --resources-vpc-config \
    subnetIds=subnet-6782e71e,subnet-e7e761ac,securityGroupIds=sg-6979fe18
```

where, once again, AWS concepts such as IAM roles, subnet IDs, and security groups leak through. Admittedly, much of this will be prepopulated if you create the cluster through the AWS Console; however, these settings can certainly be scary and a bit off-putting to the uninitiated. That said, we do end up with a high availability cluster spread across different Availability Zones (AZs).

EKS tends to work out pricier than the other offerings, in part because Amazon charges a $0.20/hour fee per cluster for the management layer.

Azure Kubernetes Service

Azure Kubernetes Service (AKS)[28] is a solid contender, but probably is a runner-up to GKE in terms of features and ease of use.

Here's the command to create a cluster for comparison:

```
az aks create \
    --name myAKSCluster \
    --resource-group myResourceGroup \
    --node-count 1 \
    --generate-ssh-keys \
    --service-principal <appId> \
    --client-secret <password>
```

The field is changing fast, so AKS is definitely one to watch.

Choosing Between These CaaS Platforms

If you're deciding between these platforms, there are plenty of good articles on the relative merits of each.[29]

Amazon is the oddity in the group. ECS has a proprietary orchestration layer, and EKS requires more manual work to get your clusters up and running. Both expose AWS-specific internals, giving you more flexibility at the expense of the ease of use you'd typically expect from a managed service.

---

28. https://azure.microsoft.com/en-gb/services/kubernetes-service/
29. https://blog.hasura.io/gke-vs-aks-vs-eks-411f080640dc

The main reasons to go with Amazon's platforms are if you:

- Are already heavily invested in AWS
- Want to integrate with your existing AWS infrastructure
- Want to integrate with other AWS services
- Have a lot of AWS experience on the team
- Want to build something extremely custom

If you have no existing baggage and just want to get up and running fast, I'd recommend Google Kubernetes Engine as a starting point. It seems to be the most mature offering, and Kubernetes started life at Google.

Serverless for Containers

Much fuss has been made about the name *serverless computing*,[30,31,32] but putting that aside, there's a growing demand for ever-more-abstracted services.

Popularized by services like Amazon's AWS Lambda,[33] Serverless Computing has become synonymous with Functions as a Service (FAAS). You supply some code to be run when a particular event occurs, and the platform takes care of how and where it's run. Although the code you supply is typically turned into containers behind the scenes, that's an implementation detail you don't need to care about. The benefit to this computing model is that you completely remove the need to provision infrastructure, and scaling happens automatically based on load.

However, a major downside is that you are limited by the languages and tooling supported by the FAAS platform.[34] If, instead of supplying raw code files, you provide your own Docker images, you get all the benefits of FAAS, but with fewer runtime limitations. Rather than being constrained by the platform, you have full control over what languages and tooling your code uses.

Sound too good to be true? Well, the future is already here—at least, a limited version of it. There are only two offerings so far, but no doubt more will gradually appear, and the services will continue to mature.

---

30. https://twitter.com/thepracticaldev/status/857075416217010178
31. https://news.ycombinator.com/item?id=14742273
32. https://hackernoon.com/what-the-hell-does-serverless-mean-219a5f6e3c6a
33. https://aws.amazon.com/lambda
34. https://docs.aws.amazon.com/lambda/latest/dg/current-supported-versions.html

AWS Fargate

AWS Fargate[35] is a new platform from Amazon that puts a serverless spin on their ECS and EKS services. Both ECS and EKS, by default, require some manual steps to create the EC2 instances that will run the containers. Fargate is a drop-in replacement compute engine for ECS and EKS that removes the need to think about and manage server instances.

How does this work in practice? You specify your containers, as well as config regarding how the containers should be managed at runtime. Based on the CPU and memory parameters you set, Fargate will automatically scale your containers up or down as necessary, based on load; you don't need to care where or how they're run.

Fargate containers can be used to run one-off, short-lived tasks—much like AWS Lambdas. In addition, Fargate is currently the only Serverless offering that supports traditional-style applications and microservices.

Although Fargate removes a lot of the orchestration burden of running containers in production, as with AWS EKS, you still have to have some interaction with underlying AWS services to configure your networking and specify security policies.

Pricing for Fargate is based on virtual CPU and memory usage, and is currently anything from two to six times more expensive than running an EC2 instance. The gap is even wider when you consider that an EC2 instance is capable of running multiple containers. So, although an interesting service to watch, the price needs to come down before it will gain real momentum.

Microsoft Azure Container Instances

Microsoft Azure Container Instances (ACI)[36] is a much more limited form of serverless for containers. It can't be used to run a standard containerized application like our Rails app we've been building throughout the book. Instead, it's intended for applications that have built from the ground up to be Serverless; it's suitable for discrete tasks (such as data processing) or event-driven applications.

As with Fargate, pricing is based on virtual CPU and memory usage, and the two services cost roughly the same.

---

35. https://aws.amazon.com/fargate/
36. https://azure.microsoft.com/en-gb/services/container-instances/

How to Decide What's Right for Me?

When it comes to choosing your production environment, there's no right answer; one size does not fit all. Rather than give you specific advice or recommendations, instead it's important to highlight some key criteria that you'll need to think about when deciding.

Here are the trade-offs to think about:

Upfront cost vs. long-term cost. The unit cost for services generally increases with the amount they manage for you; IaaS is typically cheaper than CaaS, which is cheaper than Serverless. However, the less managed, the more upfront engineering effort is required. It's often larger, more established companies that go down the IaaS route; they have the deep pockets required, and more certainty that they'll be around long enough to benefit from the multiyear cost savings. For smaller companies, and especially startups, these upfront costs are hard to justify unless they give a key competitive advantage.

Focus and developer bandwidth. Similar to cost, can you afford the time and loss of focus spent building your platform on top of IaaS, rather than just getting something working faster with a managed service? The general wisdom is that you should focus on what makes you and your product unique—in most cases, this won't be your production environment.

Support and maintenance costs. If you use a CaaS platform, the service is managed, maintained, and improved by someone else. If things go wrong, it's most likely someone else's problem to fix. If you roll your own solution, be prepared for more support and maintenance to fall on your shoulders.

Control and flexibility. With a CaaS, you have limited control to change the fundamental features or capability of the system, whereas IaaS gives you ultimate control to build systems as you like. Consider how much control you need and along what dimensions. Some industries have very specific security or audit requirements that might necessitate a bespoke solution. However, Kubernetes gives you lots of options for architecting your software, so it may provide as much flexibility as you need.

Regional availability. If you're based in Sydney and delivering software for users in Sao Paulo, to avoid high latency, your app should probably be hosted close to the end users. Some of the managed CaaS services have limited regional availability, which may rule out certain offerings.

Level of expertise required vs. ability of team. Building your own secure cloud platform, even if leveraging some good defaults that may be provided in an

IaaS, will require more specialist skills and experience from your team. If your team doesn't have these, steer clear.

Vendor/platform lock-in. Using a particular tool or service both ties you to it and frees you from something else. Adopting Kubernetes will necessarily mean thinking in its conceptual model, defining config files a certain way, and more generally, building your team's workflows around it: all forms of lock-in. On the other hand, managing apps with Kubernetes on one host will be very similar, if not the same, as on any other, so it reduces hosting platform lock-in. Similarly, building on top of IaaS gives certain freedoms, but couples you to the hosting provider. Choose your poison wisely.

Quick Recap

In this chapter, we took a step back to fill in some context around choosing your production platform, and we discussed what's involved with deploying and operating applications. Although much of this may have already been familiar to you, we took a very Docker-centric slant to understand how the production landscape differs once you've adopted Docker.

In particular:

1. We reviewed what is meant by "Ops" and explored how using Docker answers some common pieces of the puzzle.

2. We learned about orchestration tools, which provide us with a platform for creating and managing compute clusters capable of delivering and running our containerized apps in a resilient way.

3. We discussed Swarm and Kubernetes, giving a brief outline of their relative strengths and weaknesses.

4. We considered the decision of whether to build on top of an IaaS platform or go the more managed route with a CaaS provider.

5. We looked at the tools you might use to provision IaaS infrastructure.

6. We had a quick tour of some popular CaaS platforms.

7. We considered the trade-offs involved in deciding which platform and tools are right for you.

Armed with these insights, let's dive back into the practical details again, and turn our attention to prepping our app for production. Full steam ahead!

## CHAPTER 12

Preparing for Production

Ever heard the culinary term *mise en place*? Translated literally, it means *everything in its place*; it refers to the prep work done before actually starting to cook. I've watched enough *Ramsay's Kitchen Nightmares* to know that no self-respecting chef begins without it. Similarly, eager as we are to see our app running in production, there are a few preliminaries to take care of first.

In this chapter, we'll lay the groundwork for deploying to production, starting with how to configure different environments in a Docker-centric world. We'll also precompile our assets and bake them into our image, ready to be served up in production.

Finally, we'll learn how to share our custom images to make them available for use beyond our local machine.

Chopping board and peeler at the ready? Let's get to it.

Configuring a Production Environment

Rails pioneered out-of-the-box support for multiple environments. How does this fit in with our Docker setup? We know that our production config will differ from that in development, but what settings do we need and how do we organize things?

Previously, we created the following file structure for our config:

```
$ tree .env
.env
└── development
    ├── database
    └── web

1 directory, 2 files
```

Let's create a copy of our development config as a starting point for our production config:

```
$ cp -r .env/development .env/production
```

This should leave us with the following file structure:

```
$ tree .env
.env
├── development
│   ├── database
│   └── web
└── production
    ├── database
    └── web

2 directories, 4 files
```

Now let's edit the .env/production/web file to look like this:

```
DATABASE_HOST=database
RAILS_ENV=production
SECRET_KEY_BASE=
RAILS_LOG_TO_STDOUT=true
RAILS_SERVE_STATIC_FILES=true
```

We have to remember to set RAILS_ENV to production so that the app starts in production mode.

Rails uses SECRET_KEY_BASE as a security mechanism to sign the cookies it sets, allowing it to verify that cookies it receives can be trusted. We've intentionally left it blank because we need to generate a new one for our production config. Let's do that now using Rails' handy Rake task:

```
$ docker-compose exec web bin/rails secret
9d6d05e1990f81bbba154b1fc54c23c6ffaafb081a07e5ac3731160a6126e711c2f1d7623b6d
5140c03686462cda966344fe6f1b35fa44c14eaba50769692c74
```

Paste your generated secret key into your .env/production/web file as the value for the SECRET_KEY_BASE environment variable.

By default, Rails logs to a file on disk in logs/<environment>.log. In a Docker environment, we don't want the logs to be written to the filesystem *inside* the container as they're hard to get to from there. Instead, we want to configure the app to output its logs to stdout, which allows us to view the log using Docker's log commands. We can do this by setting the RAILS_LOG_TO_STDOUT environment variable (added in Rails 5) to true.

Also, we are going to have Rails serve our static assets, so we need to set RAILS_SERVE_STATIC_FILES to true to make them available in production.

Now let's edit your .env/production/database file to be as follows:

```
POSTGRES_USER=postgres
➤ POSTGRES_PASSWORD=my-production-password
➤ POSTGRES_DB=myapp_production
```

We've changed the Postgres password so that it's different from development. We've also updated the database name to be myapp_production instead of myapp_development.

Although there's more that could be tweaked, we've completed the essential configuration for production.

A Production Image: Precompiling Assets

In development, by default, Rails compiles our assets for each request so that our changes are picked up automatically. However, typically in production, we precompile our assets once and then serve them up as static files for faster load times. Rails provides the following Rake task for this:

```
bin/rails assets:precompile
```

Up until now, the changes we've needed to make for our app to run in production have just been config changes, or tweaks that would be fine in development too. Here, however, the production version of our app needs additional files: the compiled assets.

How do we achieve this with our Docker setup?

The solution is to create a second, production-flavored image that precompiles the assets at build time, so the compiled assets are baked into the image itself. Generally, it's a good idea to keep your development environment as similar to production as possible. However, some changes, like this need to precompile assets for production, require that our development and production environments diverge slightly.

Let's create a Dockerfile for our production image. Start by taking a copy:

```
$ cp Dockerfile Dockerfile.prod
```

Next, let's update our Dockerfile.prod to precompile assets by adding the following line just before the ENTRYPOINT command:

```
➤ RUN bin/rails assets:precompile
ENTRYPOINT ["./docker-entrypoint.sh"]
CMD ["bin/rails", "s", "-b", "0.0.0.0"]
```

We now have a Dockerfile to create a production version of our image. There are further enhancements that we might want to make, but it's a good start. It allows us to deploy a production version of our app and see it running. Note that we haven't built the image yet: we'll get to that shortly.

Sharing Images

Up until now, during development, we've been building our custom images on our local machine. Initially, we did this with this command:

```
$ docker build [OPTIONS] .
```

We quickly progressed to using Compose to build images for us—for example:

```
$ docker-compose build web
```

However, we have a problem. We're going to need to run those same images we've been building locally on *different machines* as our app progresses through our build pipeline environments (such as testing, integration, staging, and production). How will we get our images onto the different machines?

One possibility is to rebuild the image on each machine that needs it, but this is wasteful and time-consuming. Images are more than just a convenient way to package up our code to be run in isolated containers. Since they contain everything needed to run the software, they are the perfect unit for sharing.

Docker has a built-in mechanism for distributing images. In fact, we've already seen it in action. Think back, for example, to one of our first Docker commands:

```
$ docker run ruby:2.6 ruby -e "puts :hello"
```

When we tried to run a container based on the ruby:2.6 image, Docker detected that we didn't have that image locally, and proceeded to download it.

```
Unable to find image 'ruby:2.6' locally
2.6: Pulling from library/ruby
cd8eada9c7bb: Pull complete
c2677faec825: Pull complete
fcce419a96b1: Pull complete
045b51e26e75: Pull complete
3b969ad6f147: Pull complete
f2db762ad32e: Pull complete
708e57760f1b: Pull complete
06478b05a41b: Pull complete
Digest: sha256:ad724f6982b4a7c2d2a8a4ecb67267a1961a518029244ed943e2d448d6fb7
994
Status: Downloaded newer image for ruby:2.6
hello
```

We want this capability for our own images.

If you think about it, this mechanism presupposes that images are hosted somewhere: somewhere that Docker knows to find them.

Enter Docker Registries.

Much like you'd share a Git repo by pushing it to a centralized hosting service like GitHub, we can share our Docker images by pushing them to a centralized Docker image-hosting service—or in Docker parlance, *Docker Registries*.

Docker provides its own hosted Registry called Docker Hub,[1] which with a free account, gives you unlimited public repos and one private repo. For more private repos, you can sign up for one of its paid plans.[2] However, as we'll see shortly, on page 152, there are other options, including hosting your own Docker Registry.[3]

For simplicity, we're going to use Docker Hub as our Registry throughout the rest of this book, so to follow along, you'll need a Docker Hub account. If you don't already have one, let's create it now.

Visit hub.docker.com in a browser, and sign up for an account. You'll need to choose a username—known as a *Docker ID*. I recommend using the same name as your GitHub account to keep things simple, although this is not necessary. Join me back here when you're done.

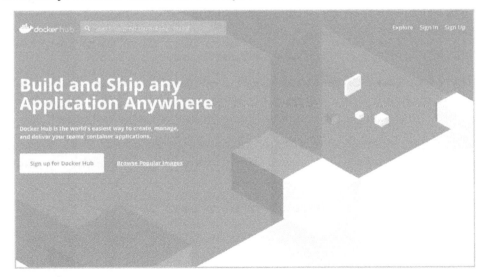

---

1. https://hub.docker.com
2. https://hub.docker.com/billing-plans/
3. https://docs.docker.com/registry/deploying/

Referring to Images Unambiguously

Previously, when we named our image on page 31, we simply called it railsapp. Similarly, Compose automatically named our web service image myapp_web. Although these names worked fine when working on a single Docker Machine, they aren't suitable for sharing our image on a Docker Registry.

Why? Because what if different people, teams, or organizations all want to have an image called railsapp or myapp_web? How would we know which image to refer to? This is a solved problem: by referring to both the image name *and* a user account, we disambiguate which image we're referring to and allow people to call their images whatever they like without fear of name clashes.

We refer, unambiguously, to a particular image (more precisely, a specific *version* of an image) by using the following naming convention:

```
[<registry hostname>[:port]/]<username>/<image name>[:<tag>]
```

The Registry hostname is optional; leaving it out indicates you're referring to the default Registry: Docker Hub. If a Registry hostname is provided without an explicit port, the standard SSL port 443 is assumed.[4]

As we'll see in a moment, an account is needed to store images on a Registry, and an account can house any number of distinctly named images. The <username>/<image name> combination refers to the particular image in a given user account. In fact, everything up until the optional tag is known as the *repository name*:

```
[<registry hostname>[:port]/]<username>/<image name>
```

A repository can store multiple tagged versions of the image; we refer to a particular version of the image either by specifying an explicit tag or, as we saw previously, on page 31 by letting the default tag—latest—be used.

For example, since my Docker Hub username is robisenberg, to share the latest version of an image called myapp_web on Docker Hub, I'd use the repository name robisenberg/myapp_web.

Repository Names in Examples

 In the commands that follow, you will need to replace my account name (robisenberg) with whatever you called yours.

4.　https://docs.docker.com/registry/deploying/#run-an-externally-accessible-registry

You may be wondering how we were able to download images like ruby:2.6, redis, and postgres that aren't fully qualified image names. Good question. Docker elevates certain popular images by calling them *Docker Official Images*. These are placed in a special, top-level namespace that lets you refer to them simply by their image name. However, for our own images, we will always need to use fully qualified image names that include our repository name.

Pushing Our Image to a Registry

Now that we have a user account and understand fully qualified image names, we're ready to share our image by *pushing* it to a Docker Registry. As we said earlier, we're going to use Docker Hub since it's free (within certain limits), requires no setup, and is the default.

Right now, we're more concerned with sharing the production (rather than development) version of our image, although sharing the development image works in exactly the same way. Bear in mind throughout this section that on a *real* project, we wouldn't build and push images ourselves from our local machine: this would happen automatically as part of our CI pipeline. However, there's no magic to it, so learning how to do this manually will put you in good stead for setting up your CI.

First, we need to tag our image with the correct repository name we want to push it to. As we saw earlier on page 31, if our image is already built, we could tag it with the command:

```
$ docker tag <image ref> robisenberg/<image_name>
```

where <image ref> is either an image ID or a name we've already given it. However, since we haven't built our production image yet, we can build and tag it in one go.

Let's do this now:

```
$ docker build -f Dockerfile.prod -t robisenberg/myapp_web:prod .
«...»
Successfully built 6828234d25af
Successfully tagged robisenberg/myapp_web:prod
```

The -f option lets us specify the name of a different filename for the Dockerfile to build the image from: in this case, our production image (Dockerfile.prod). As we've seen previously, the -t option tags the image with robisenberg/myapp_web:prod; this indicates the repository robisenberg/myapp_web on Docker Hub and a specific tag of prod.

OK, now that we have an image correctly tagged with the correct repository name, the next step is to *push* our image to our Docker Hub repository. However, before we can do this, we must first log in to our Docker Hub account from the CLI. Run the following command, and enter your (Docker Hub) username and password when prompted:

```
$ docker login
Login with your Docker ID to push and pull images from Docker Hub. If you
don't have a Docker ID, head over to https://hub.docker.com to create one.
Username: robisenberg
Password:
Login Succeeded
```

Having logged in successfully, we can now push our image to our Docker Hub account by issuing:

```
$ docker push robisenberg/myapp_web:prod
The push refers to repository [docker.io/robisenberg/myapp_web]
e596ed08a285: Pushed
ba1dbb2e536f: Pushed
68de2d8742b3: Pushed
58c9140d449b: Pushed
3261213dc16c: Pushed
7dc2478de08a: Pushed
5f96433196b2: Pushed
a102504f2bb1: Pushed
713891529def: Pushed
723beaa0cfe6: Layer already exists
c273f4e91860: Layer already exists
a334a91e3fd1: Layer already exists
1a36262221c3: Layer already exists
d2217ead3a1c: Layer already exists
b53b57a50746: Layer already exists
d2518892581f: Layer already exists
c581f4ede92d: Layer already exists
prod: digest: sha256:83148118939d4ae1b992e70ee08d0c155325e5c4dfed9f270dd8473
ec3a56e0a size: 3897
```

Let's verify our image has been pushed to Docker Hub. Visit hub.docker.com and log in to your account. You should see it listed there as shown in the figure on page 153.

With our image now hosted on Docker Hub, we could run this image on any Internet-connected machine with Docker installed, and just like with our ruby:2.6 hello example, our image would be downloaded automatically.

Before we conclude this chapter, consider one final point. You may not want to share your Docker images with the world. Just like you can have private Git repos, Docker Hub lets you have private image repos. Although, by default,

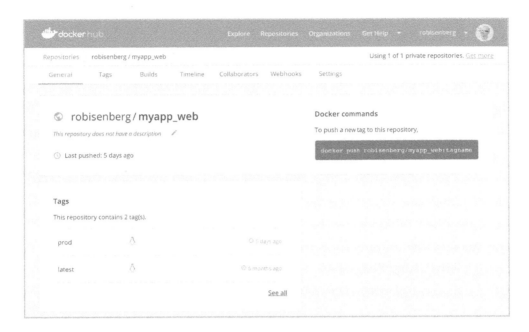

the image we pushed was public, there's a setting to make this private (we could have created a private repo first through the interface too).

In fact, there are lots of options when it comes to sharing your images, depending on your requirements. Docker Hub is only one of several hosted registries available. Other options include:

- Amazon Elastic Container Registry[5]
- Google Cloud Container Registry[6]
- Microsoft Azure Container Registry[7]
- Quay[8]

For security (or other) reasons, some organizations may need to host their own internal Docker Registries. Docker Registry is an open source project[9] that you can run on your own infrastructure.[10] Another good option is Harbor,[11] a more fully featured Docker Registry under the care of the CNCF.[12]

---

5. https://aws.amazon.com/ecr/
6. https://cloud.google.com/container-registry/
7. https://azure.microsoft.com/en-gb/services/container-registry/
8. https://quay.io
9. https://github.com/docker/distribution
10. https://docs.docker.com/registry/deploying/
11. https://goharbor.io/
12. https://www.cncf.io

Quick Recap

Ahh, that's better; we can hang up our apron. Our preparation—or *mise en place*—is complete.

Let's review what we covered in this chapter:

1. We configured our app to run in production, with the necessary environment variables set.

2. We created an enhanced production image that precompiled our assets.

3. We discussed the need for making our images available on different machines, and you learned how Docker Registries facilitate this.

4. We saw the naming convention we need to refer to a specific version of an image unambiguously:

    ```
    [<registry hostname>[:port]/]<username>/<image name>[:<tag>]
    ```

5. You created a Docker Hub account (if you didn't already have one).

6. We built our production image and pushed it to a public Docker Registry (Docker Hub), making it available for download on our production machines.

With our production config in place and image pushed to Docker Hub, we're ready to start deploying our app to production-like environments.

## CHAPTER 13

A Production-Like Playground

We're *so* close. In the previous chapter, we configured our application so it's ready to run in production environments, and we pushed our image to Docker Hub. However, before we start setting up cloud-based infrastructure and deploying it there, we're first going to get our sea legs, so to speak, by having a practice run locally.

In this chapter, we'll make use of virtualization technologies—specifically, VirtualBox—to create virtual infrastructure on our local machine that can simulate a production environment. We'll create a single node cluster, capable of running Docker containers. Not only will we deploy our application, we'll also see how to scale up the app and run multiple copies of it on this single instance.

In the process, we'll learn about the additional tools Docker provides for creating infrastructure, and deploying and managing production apps. Although we're working locally, the skills will translate directly to doing these same things on cloud-based infrastructure.

Creating Machines

If we're going to deploy our application in production, we need to have somewhere to deploy it to. That means, infrastructure: machine instances capable of running code.

As we saw in Chapter 11, *The Production Landscape*, on page 129, there are a number of tools available for creating and configuring our infrastructure. However, since this is a book about Docker, we're going to stick with Docker's own tool—Docker Machine—for handling this.

Docker Machine is a command-line tool that can create Docker-ready instances for us. It uses the adapter pattern, providing a number of different *drivers*[1] capable of creating instances on different platforms. This means we can use similar commands to create instances, whether they're virtual instances running on our local machine or cloud-based infrastructure.

In this chapter, we're going to use VirtualBox to run our local instances. If you don't already have it and want to follow along, you'll have to install it. VirtualBox's documentation[2] is pretty comprehensive. Go to the installation section[3] and follow the instructions for whichever platform you're running. Meet me back here when you're done.

Windows 10: Hyper-V or VirtualBox?

If you installed Docker via Docker for Windows—which relies on Microsoft *Hyper-V*— you will need to use Hyper-V instead of VirtualBox for local virtualization. Make sure you have Hyper-V set up correctly to work with Docker Machine as per Docker's example.[4]

Unlike VirtualBox users, you will need to use a command like this to create a machine with Hyper-V:

```
$ docker-machine create \
    --driver hyperv \
    --hyperv-virtual-switch "myswitch" \
    local-vm-1
```

All set? Great.

Now that you have VirtualBox running, we can create a new virtual machine for running our app:

```
$ docker-machine create --driver virtualbox local-vm-1
Running pre-create checks...
Creating machine...
(local-vm-1) Copying /Users/rob/.docker/machine/cache/boot2docker.iso to
/Users/rob/.docker/machine/machines/local-vm-1/boot2docker.iso...
(local-vm-1) Creating VirtualBox VM...
(local-vm-1) Creating SSH key...
(local-vm-1) Starting the VM...
(local-vm-1) Check network to re-create if needed...
(local-vm-1) Waiting for an IP...
Waiting for machine to be running, this may take a few minutes...
```

---

1. https://docs.docker.com/machine/drivers/
2. https://www.virtualbox.org/manual/
3. https://www.virtualbox.org/manual/ch02.html
4. docs.docker.com/machine/drivers/hyper-v/#example

```
Detecting operating system of created instance...
Waiting for SSH to be available...
Detecting the provisioner...
Provisioning with boot2docker...
Copying certs to the local machine directory...
Copying certs to the remote machine...
Setting Docker configuration on the remote daemon...
Checking connection to Docker...
Docker is up and running!
To see how to connect your Docker Client to the Docker Engine running on
this virtual machine, run: docker-machine env local-vm-1
```

This command says, "Create a VirtualBox instance named local-vm-1." The output shows the various steps it goes through to provision our instance. You can see, for example, that it uses an image called boot2docker.iso; boot2docker is a lightweight Linux distro that's optimized for running Docker.

We can verify our instance has been created by listing the instances that docker-machine knows about:

```
$ docker-machine ls
NAME        ACTIVE DRIVER     STATE   URL         SWARM DOCKER     ERRORS
local-vm-1 -       virtualbox Running tcp://19…           v18.09.1
```

What can we do with our new instance? Let's take it for a little spin.

For a start, we can SSH onto it:

```
$ docker-machine ssh local-vm-1
   ( '>')
  /) TC (\    Core is distributed with ABSOLUTELY NO WARRANTY.
 (/-_--_-\)            www.tinycorelinux.net
docker@local-vm-1:~$
```

We can see that Docker is installed:

```
docker@local-vm-1:~$ docker -v
Docker version 18.09.1, build 4c52b90
```

Having SSH'd onto the machine, we could issue our Docker commands directly here to start Docker services on this new host.

Alternatively, if we exit this SSH session and return to our local machine:

```
docker@local-vm-1:~$ exit
```

we can then issue commands against this new instance by specifying a command string at the end of the SSH command:

```
$ docker-machine ssh <instance name> "<command>"
```

This runs the command on the instance by logging in with SSH. Typically, this is more convenient for one-off commands to avoid having to SSH in and terminate a session manually.

Let's try this now:

```
$ docker-machine ssh local-vm-1 "echo 'hello'"
hello
```

As you can see, this ran the command on our local VirtualBox instance and displayed the output.

Configuring the Docker CLI

There's yet another way to perform actions on our docker-machine-managed instance: we can configure our (local) Docker client to talk to our new instance's Docker Engine. This is a huge benefit of Docker's client-server architecture we saw earlier on page 13. We can use the same commands with the client CLI locally and have it take effect on any remote machine of our choosing; we simply configure our CLI to point to different machines.

Configuring the Docker CLI to point at a different instance's Docker Engine is done via environment variables. However, we don't have to manage them manually; Docker Machine provides a shortcut. If you look back at the output when we created our new instance, the final line said:

```
To see how to connect your Docker Client to the Docker Engine running on
this virtual machine, run: docker-machine env local-vm-1
```

Let's run this now:

```
$ docker-machine env local-vm-1
export DOCKER_TLS_VERIFY="1"
export DOCKER_HOST="tcp://192.168.99.100:2376"
export DOCKER_CERT_PATH="/Users/rob/.docker/machine/machines/local-vm-1"
export DOCKER_MACHINE_NAME="local-vm-1"
# Run this command to configure your shell:
# eval $(docker-machine env local-vm-1)
```

This command prints the environment variables that must be set, but doesn't actually set them. To set them, we can follow the instructions in the output and run:

```
$ eval $(docker-machine env local-vm-1)
```

Our current terminal session is now configured so our Docker commands will run on our new, virtual instance, rather than our normal Docker installation.

To verify this, we can rerun:

```
$ docker-machine ls
NAME        ACTIVE DRIVER     STATE    URL        SWARM DOCKER      ERRORS
local-vm-1 *       virtualbox Running  tcp://19…        v18.09.1
```

You can see there's a star in the "Active" column for our new instance. If we were using our local Docker Engine, this would instead be -.

What does this mean in practice? All our standard Docker commands will now apply and run against our new VirtualBox instance. For example, if we list our images, rather than outputting the various images we know we have on our local Docker installation, we get an empty list:

```
$ docker images
REPOSITORY    TAG    IMAGE ID    CREATED    SIZE
```

That's because, on our new instance, no images have been built or pulled down yet.

This leads to an important question: how do we get images on the new instance? You may already know, but let's answer this by rerunning our very first Docker command in the book, but this time, let's target our new instance:

```
$ docker run ruby:2.6 ruby -e "puts :hello"
Unable to find image 'ruby:2.6' locally
2.6: Pulling from library/ruby
cd8eada9c7bb: Pull complete
c2677faec825: Pull complete
fcce419a96b1: Pull complete
045b51e26e75: Pull complete
3b969ad6f147: Pull complete
f2db762ad32e: Pull complete
708e57760f1b: Pull complete
06478b05a41b: Pull complete
Digest: sha256:ad724f6982b4a7c2d2a8a4ecb67267a1961a518029244ed943e2d448d6fb7
994
Status: Downloaded newer image for ruby:2.6
hello
```

Running this command causes Docker to pull down the ruby:2.6 image on our new instance, so now when we list the images again, we can see it there:

```
$ docker images
REPOSITORY    TAG    IMAGE ID       CREATED       SIZE
ruby          2.6    f28a9e1d0449   6 days ago    868MB
```

Having configured our Docker CLI to point to the new instance, we can run Docker commands locally and have them seamlessly take effect on the remote instance. Images that aren't available on the remote instance will be downloaded as needed, just like they were locally.

Introducing Docker Swarm

Remember, we're treating this virtual instance as if it were a production instance for our application. Our objective is to start our application on this instance so that it can be used to service real requests.

There are number of ways you could do this. For example, you *could* use low-level Docker commands to start the various containers for our application. However, having created a nice abstraction for our application with our docker-compose.yml file, that doesn't sound appealing. If you're thinking that we could use Compose directly to manage our app on this new instance, you're close to where we're headed.

The truth, though, is that Compose, as a tool, is really designed to help us during *development*. Once we get to a production environment, we have a whole different set of concerns that didn't really affect us in development, such as:

- How do we make our app resilient to failures?
- How can we scale our application to handle varying load?
- How do we deploy new versions of our application with no (or minimal) downtime for users?

Instead, as we saw earlier on page 133, Docker provides a container *orchestrator*, Swarm, for managing apps in production.

Using Swarm (the tool), you create clusters—*swarms*— of one or more connected instances; these work as a single, resilient unit on which to run services in containers. Swarm is declarative: we tell it the state we want our application to be in, and it pulls the various knobs and levers to make this happen. As you'd hope, it leverages the docker-compose.yml format that we've used to specify our application.

Our First (Single Node) Swarm

It's time to dive deeper into Swarm and start getting our hands dirty.

Previously, we created a plain-vanilla Docker instance: local-vm-1. To turn our instance into a swarm, we have to initialize it explicitly. With our CLI targeting our new instance, we can do this by running:

```
$ docker swarm init --advertise-addr <IP address of instance>
```

where <IP address of instance>, in our case, is local-vm-1's public IP address. We can easily find that out by rerunning:

```
$ docker-machine ls
NAME           ...  ...  ...    URL                          ...  ...  ...
local-vm-1  *  ...  ...         tcp://192.168.99.100:2376         ...
```

The IP address of the instance is listed in the "URL" column. For me, the IP address is 192.168.99.100, but yours will differ.

Let's go ahead and run this now (substituting the correct IP):

```
$ docker swarm init --advertise-addr 192.168.99.100
Swarm initialized: current node (kun8mrdiuhewsydse3exvdq4a) is now a manager

To add a worker to this swarm, run the following command:

    docker swarm join --token SWMTKN-1-64vcnpwr3sv6pco6ha8fyzm3pbi71h72cqq89
owty12uvlrd80-a0g240eqg899rbidxnw7q3fa4 192.168.99.100:2377

To add a manager to this swarm, run 'docker swarm join-token manager' and
follow the instructions.
```

For now, we're going to stick with a single-node Swarm cluster. However, you'll notice in the output instructions for connecting more instances to the swarm—we'll come back to this later.

OK, single-node swarm at the ready. How do we deploy our application to it?

Describing Our App to Swarm

You're probably becoming pretty comfortable describing our app as a set of services defined in a Compose file. However, a docker-compose.yml file is *development-focused*; it lets us rebuild images easily and not get bogged down in unnecessary details such as deployment configuration. However, now when we come to deployment, we need something that is *deployment-focused*.

Swarm introduces the concept of a *stack* to mean an application made up of a group of services that are *capable of being deployed*. We describe our stack to Swarm with a deployment-focused variant of a Compose file known as a *stack* file. Although you'll sometimes still hear this referred to as a Compose file, we'll stick with the latter since it clearly distinguishes it from a normal Compose file.

Ready to create your first stack file? Copy our docker-compose.yml file to one called docker-stack.yml, then modify it so it looks as follows:

```
Line 1   version: '3'

   -     services:
   -       web:
   5           image: robisenberg/myapp_web:prod
   -           ports:
   -             - "80:3000"
   -           env_file:
   -             - .env/production/database
   10            - .env/production/web

   -         redis:
   -           image: redis

   15        database:
   -           image: postgres
   -           env_file:
   -             - .env/production/database
   -           volumes:
   20            - db_data:/var/lib/postgresql/data

   -     volumes:
   -       db_data:
```

You'll notice a number of changes. For a start, we've completely removed the webpack_dev_server and selenium_chrome services: these were only needed for development and testing.

The remaining changes relate to the web service. We've removed the build attribute from the web service since building an image from a Dockerfile only works with Compose; with Swarm, we must specify a preexisting image to use. Here we specify the fully qualified name for the production image we pushed to Docker Hub: robisenberg/myapp_web:prod (line 5); in particular, we specify the version of this image tagged as prod.

We've also removed the web service's volumes attribute, which we previously used to mount our local Rails folder into the container (for live code reloading) and mount our gem cache (to speed up gem changes). Since we won't be developing or changing the code in production, neither of these are necessary.

We've changed the env_files to point to our production config (lines 9–10).

Finally, we've changed the mapped port for the web service so it exposes the Rails server on the default HTTP port 80 (line 7).

There are lots more options and features we could use,[5] but this basic docker-stack.yml file is a good starting point. However, before we can use it to deploy our app, we need to make some changes to it to set up our database.

Migrating the Database

We saw on page 78 that the Postgres image automatically creates the default database if it doesn't exist. However, currently nothing ensures that the migrations have been run; in development, we just did this manually. We need to ensure that our app has a fully migrated database when it launches.

One way you *might* think of achieving this is with the entrypoint concept we introduced on page 121 to solve the server PID issue. We already have a docker-entrypoint.sh file that is run just prior to launching our app; this might lead you to try migrating the database as follows:

```
#!/bin/sh

set -e

if [ -f tmp/pids/server.pid ]; then
  rm tmp/pids/server.pid
fi

# BAD IDEA...
bin/rails db:migrate

exec "$@"
```

Although it seems like this approach *should* work, unfortunately it doesn't scale well. Were you to start three replicas of your app at the same time, each would try to migrate the database, which can lead to locking issues that prevent the app from starting. Another downside is that you can't migrate the database *independently*; it is tied to the app launch.

A better solution is to create a separate *service* whose sole responsibility is to migrate the database. Unlike our other services which are long-lived, this would be a *one-shot container*[6]—it would execute a single command that is expected to terminate (we'll see how to declare this shortly). The nice thing about this approach is that it gives us fine-grained control to migrate our production database at any point, just by relaunching the db-migrator service. However, it also introduces a challenge.

---

5. https://docs.docker.com/compose/compose-file/#deploy
6. https://blog.alexellis.io/containers-on-swarm/

Let's think about timing for a moment. Unlike our redis and database services, which have no dependencies, our web service relies on the database service being available in order to start successfully (it also relies on redis, but as we only connect in a controller, this wouldn't cause an error at startup). However, the *order* that services launch is indeterminate; it is affected by image size, download speeds, load, and, importantly, how long it takes for the container's command to have performed any initialization. What happens if our web service launches before the database service is ready for connections?

We have largely been shielded from having to care about this lack of determinism because—thanks to Swarm's default behavior—our web service automatically restarts if it fails to launch for any reason, including being unable to connect to the database. However, using a one-shot container changes things. If our planned database-migrator service launched before Postgres was ready for connections, it would fail with a PG::ConnectionBad error, and terminate. Our one-shot container would have missed its one chance, leaving our database unmigrated. Not a pretty sight.

Generally, we should design our apps to be resilient to services coming and going, and not being available when expected.[7] Here, a good solution is to wrap the rails db:migrate command with a script that waits until the database is not just started, but ready to handle connections. You can think of this as a *readiness health check*. We're going to use a shell script called wait-for[8] to perform this checking for us.

Download the wait-for script in your Rails root folder.

We'll need to include this file in our myapp_web:prod image, so we'll rebuild the image shortly. However, the wait-for script relies on having the netcat Unix tool[9] available in order to determine whether the database is accepting connections on its designated port, so we'll need to install that too.

Modify your Dockerfile.prod file to add netcat to the apt-get install command:

```
RUN apt-get update -yqq && apt-get install -yqq --no-install-recommends \
  netcat \ # needed for `wait-for` TCP connection checking
  nodejs \
  yarn
```

We also need to make the wait-for script executable inside the image. On Linux or macOS, you can do this by running chmod +x wait-for locally; the file will

---

7.   https://docs.docker.com/compose/startup-order/

8.   https://github.com/mrako/wait-for

9.   https://en.wikipedia.org/wiki/Netcat

retain its execute permissions when added to the image. However, this won't work on Windows because file permissions are handled differently. Instead, we can set this file's permission in our Dockerfile.prod file itself (it's not a bad thing for this to be explicit anyway, whichever platform you're on):

```
COPY . /usr/src/app/
➤ RUN ["chmod", "+x", "/usr/src/app/wait-for"]
```

OK, time to rebuild our image. Remember, though, that our Docker Engine is currently targeting local-vm-1. Since this VM is simulating our production environment, it doesn't make sense to rebuild our image there; we normally build images either locally or as part of our CI pipeline. So let's quickly switch back to targeting our local Docker Engine:

```
$ eval $(docker-machine env -u)
```

Now let's rebuild our image with these changes and push it to DockerHub:

```
$ docker build -f Dockerfile.prod -t robisenberg/myapp_web:prod .
$ docker push robisenberg/myapp_web:prod
```

Now we're ready to define our one-shot db-migrator service in our docker-stack.yml file:

```
Line 1  db-migrator:
    2    image: robisenberg/myapp_web:prod
    3    command: ["./wait-for", "--timeout=300", "database:5432", "--",
    4              "bin/rails", "db:migrate"]
    5    env_file:
    6      - .env/production/database
    7      - .env/production/web
    8    deploy:
    9      restart_policy:
   10        condition: none
```

The command (lines 3–4) says, "Wait for up to 5 mins (300 seconds) until the host called database is accepting connections on port 5432, and as soon as it's available, run the command bin/rails db:migrate." This means that our database will be migrated successfully even if it takes a considerable time for the database to become available.

The restart_policy (line 9) prevents Swarm from trying to restart it once it has terminated; this setting is what gives the service its one-shot nature.

Sorted. Now our app can be deployed with the database fully migrated.

Deploying Our App on a Swarm

With our newly created docker-stack.yml, we have a description of our app that Swarm can use. We're ready to deploy our app onto our (single-node) swarm.

First, we must remember to retarget our swarm:

```
$ eval $(docker-machine env local-vm-1)
```

Now we can deploy our app with the command:

```
$ docker stack deploy -c docker-stack.yml myapp
Creating network myapp_default
Creating service myapp_web
Creating service myapp_redis
Creating service myapp_database
Creating service myapp_db-migrator
```

This says, "Deploy the services described in docker-stack.yml as a stack called myapp." You can see the various services being created.

We can list the services in our stack by running:

```
$ docker stack services myapp
ID    NAME                MODE   REP…  IMAGE                   PORTS
p9…   myapp_db-migrator   rep…   0/1   robisenberg/myapp_w…
s5…   myapp_web           rep…   1/1   robisenberg/myapp_w…    *:80->3000/tcp
ue…   myapp_database      rep…   1/1   postgres:latest
ws…   myapp_redis         rep…   1/1   redis:latest
```

Services deployed on Swarm can be scaled up by creating additional *replica* containers for the service. The "replicas" column shows how many replicas are running vs. the desired number of replicas (which, by default, is one).

When you run this command, you'll probably find that one or more of our services haven't started up yet, indicated by "0/1" in the "replicas" column. It may take a while until all the services have started, especially on the very first deploy, since each service's image needs to be downloaded from scratch. Wait until all the services except db-migrator have started by rerunning the command and waiting until the "replicas" column shows "1/1" (db-migrator runs and then terminates).

As a shortcut, you can also run the similar command:

```
$ docker service ls
ID    NAME                MODE   REP…  IMAGE                   PORTS
ue…   myapp_database      rep…   1/1   postgres:latest
p9…   myapp_db-migrator   rep…   0/1   robisenberg/myapp_w…
ws…   myapp_redis         rep…   1/1   redis:latest
s5…   myapp_web           rep…   1/1   robisenberg/myapp_w…    *:80->3000/tcp
```

This lists all the services that have been deployed to the swarm. With multiple stacks deployed on the swarm, you'd see the services for all stacks listed here. However, since we only have a single stack deployed, the output is the same as for docker stack services myapp, which lists the services for a *specific* stack.

OK, now that the services are running, we should be able to load our app in a browser. On your local machine, visit http://<instance IP address>/welcome, which for me is http://192.168.99.100/welcome (if you've forgotten the IP address of your instance, you can get it by running docker-machine ls). You should see our hit counter running correctly and incrementing on each page load. This shows that Redis is running and our app is connected to it successfully.

Similarly, visit http://<instance IP address>/users (for me, it's http://192.168.99.100/users), and you'll see our User scaffold showing that our database is running and our app is connected to it successfully.

We've now successfully deployed our application to the separate VirtualBox instance, which constitutes our single-node swarm cluster.

Tasks and Swarm's Scaling Model

Services running on Swarm are self-regulating. That is, we define a *desired state* for a service in terms of the number of containers that should run for it, and Swarm acts to ensure that this state is achieved and maintained.

It is this self-regulation that is key to how scaling is implemented, as well as Swarm's self-healing properties, which we'll see in the next chapter.

Swarm is made up of different parts. We can consider one part to be the *orchestrator*. Having told Swarm to deploy a service, the orchestrator is responsible for determining whether the service is in the desired state and, if not, taking action to correct this.

If the orchestrator sees that an additional container is needed, it creates a *task*, which represents the desire for a container to exist. It then sees what nodes are available in the cluster, and allocates the task to a node.

In our single-node cluster, the orchestrator has no choice but to allocate all of the tasks onto our only node. However, you can imagine that, in a multinode setup, tasks could be allocated evenly across multiple instances in the cluster.

Nodes in the cluster check with the orchestrator to know what tasks they've been allocated. They are then responsible for creating one container per task, thus achieving the desired state of the system.

An example should make this clearer. When we deployed our web service, we didn't specify the number of replica containers needed, so the default of one was assumed. The orchestrator sees that we want one web service container running, but that, initially, none are. It creates a task for the web service and assigns it to our node. The node sees that it has been allocated a web service task, and it launches a web container, meeting our desired state.

We can list the tasks in a stack with the following command:

```
$ docker stack ps myapp
ID    NAME                 IMAGE     …  DESIRED…  CURRENT…  …  …
qo…   myapp_db-migrator…   robise…   …  Shutdown  Complet…
ic…   myapp_database.1     postgr…   …  Running   Running…
8a…   myapp_redis.1        redis:…   …  Running   Running…
iw…   myapp_web.1          robise…   …  Running   Running…
```

The listing also tells us the current state of the task, whether that's successfully "Running," in the process of being started (such as "Pending" or "Preparing"), or in a number of other possible states.[10]

We can also list the tasks for a specific service. For example, to see the tasks running for our myapp_web service, we'd do:

```
$ docker service ps myapp_web
```

Scaling Up the Service

Currently, each of our services has been backed by a single task (and therefore container). We can instruct Swarm to increase or decrease the number of containers backing a service—known as scaling the service.

From the previous discussion, it should be clear how Swarm implements scaling. Imagine that the swarm receives a new definition of the web service, which specifies three containers. The orchestrator sees that only one task has been scheduled, and that therefore two more containers are required. It proceeds to create two new tasks, scheduling them across the available nodes in the cluster. The node (or nodes) allocate the tasks, then start up one container for each task they've been assigned. And voilà, we have scaled up our service to three containers.

OK, enough theory, let's see this in action.

Updating Our App

If we scale our app currently, it will be hard to tell the difference. How will we know that requests are being handled by different containers? Let's first make some changes to our app that will make this more obvious.

Edit app/controllers/welcome_controller.rb to look as follows:

---

10. https://docs.docker.com/engine/swarm/how-swarm-mode-works/swarm-task-states/

```ruby
class WelcomeController < ApplicationController
  def index
    redis = Redis.new(host: "redis", port: 6379)
    redis.incr "page hits"

    @page_hits = redis.get "page hits"
➤   @hostname = Socket.gethostname
  end
end
```

Now let's output the hostname in our view (app/views/welcome/index.html.erb):

```erb
<% content_for :head do %>
  <script type="text/javascript">
    document.addEventListener("DOMContentLoaded",function(){
      document.getElementsByTagName('h1')[0].append(' ENHANCED!');
    });
  </script>
<% end %>

<h1>This page has been viewed <%= pluralize(@page_hits, 'time') %>!</h1>
➤ <p>Request handled by host: <b><%= @hostname %></b></p>
```

We've changed our code, so we need to rebuild our image. However, remember that our Docker CLI is currently configured to target our VirtualBox instance. Really, we should switch back to our local Docker installation to build the image, rather than using the swarm instance. Typically, you won't have to remember this, as the images can be built as part of your continuous integration/continuous delivery (CI/CD) pipeline.

Let's switch our Docker CLI back to targeting commands at our local Docker installation. We do this by running:

```
$ eval $(docker-machine env -u)
```

This unsets the environment variables that we'd previously set, which made our Docker CLI target our Docker Machine–created VirtualBox instance.

Now we're good to rebuild our image:

```
$ docker build -f Dockerfile.prod -t robisenberg/myapp_web:prod .
«...»
Successfully built dd61876489b2
Successfully tagged robisenberg/myapp_web:prod
```

As we saw previously, the next step is to push our updated image to a Docker Registry—in our case, Docker Hub:

```
$ docker push robisenberg/myapp_web:prod
```

Now let's switch back to targeting our VirtualBox swarm instance:

```
$ eval $(docker-machine env local-vm-1)
```

Now we can update our web service. The easiest way to do this is simply to redeploy the stack. Swarm checks the Docker Registry for the latest versions of any images specified, and updates the services to use these versions:

```
$ docker stack deploy -c docker-stack.yml myapp
Updating service myapp_database (id: uebqig2as2r5purj7jj578brq)
Updating service myapp_db-migrator (id: p9qxhekimvz7x9glgd8pt7x5c)
Updating service myapp_web (id: s5e5ka2xss1p4yrm2rjrz9ci8)
Updating service myapp_redis (id: ws7b498dfpxxeninbgeo191qq)
```

You can also update a service's image with:

```
$ docker service update --image robisenberg/myapp_web:prod myapp_web
myapp_web
overall progress: 1 out of 1 tasks
1/1: running    [==================================================>]
verify: Service converged
```

Now view the page http://<instance IP address>/welcome (for me, 192.168.99.100/welcome). You should now see the hostname of the container running the web service. For me, it's c1ca8a915a90, but yours will differ.

Refresh the page a few times: you'll see that it's always the same hostname (because we have only one production task running it).

Scaling the App

OK, we're about to scale the app. Let's recap what the service listing shows:

```
$ docker service ls
ID    NAME                 MODE   REP… IMAGE                    PORTS
ue…   myapp_database       rep…   1/1  postgres:latest
p9…   myapp_db-migrator    rep…   1/1  robisenberg/myapp_w…
ws…   myapp_redis          rep…   1/1  redis:latest
s5…   myapp_web            rep…   1/1  robisenberg/myapp_w…     *:80->3000/tcp
```

We have a single container for the myapp_web service (replicas 1/1).

Now let's scale up our service:

```
$ docker service scale myapp_web=3
myapp_web scaled to 3
overall progress: 3 out of 3 tasks
1/3: running    [==================================================>]
2/3: running    [==================================================>]
3/3: running    [==================================================>]
verify: Service converged
```

If we check again, we'll see that the web service has three replicas running:

```
$ docker service ls
ID    NAME               MODE  REP…  IMAGE                  PORTS
ue…   myapp_database     rep…  1/1   postgres:latest
p9…   myapp_db-migrator  rep…  0/1   robisenberg/myapp_w…
ws…   myapp_redis        rep…  1/1   redis:latest
s5…   myapp_web          rep…  3/3   robisenberg/myapp_w…   *:80->3000/tcp
```

So we now have three containers each running a copy of our Rails app. Swarm load balances between replicas of your service, distributing requests to the service across the containers backing that service. However, the load balancing is nondeterministic, and Swarm can send requests to whichever container it sees fit.

Now for the real test: let's see this load balancing in action. Refresh the page http://<instance IP address>/welcome. As you refresh the page several times, you should see the hostname changing, indicating that different containers are handling the request.

You may find that the hostnames don't change when refreshing in a browser; this is likely due to browsers reusing TCP connections across multiple requests. You could try pressing and holding the keyboard shortcut for refresh (Ctrl-R or Cmd-R)—this will reload the page quickly multiple times, which allows you to see the hostname changing.

Alternatively, fetching the page with curl shows you the hostname changing as you make multiple requests:

```
$ curl -4 http://localhost:3000/welcome
```

Note: the -4 here is telling curl to use IPv4.

Swarm gives you the freedom to scale your web app however you'd like by setting the desired number of containers:

```
$ docker service scale myapp_web=<n>
```

Quick Recap

Another action-packed chapter. You've now learned the major tools in our belt for deploying apps with Docker.

Let's review what we covered in this chapter:

1. We introduced Docker Machine and used it to create a virtualized Docker-ready instance:

   ```
   $ docker-machine create --driver virtualbox local-vm-1
   ```

2. We logged onto the new instance using SSH:

```
$ docker-machine ssh local-vm-1
```

and issued commands against it from our local shell session:

```
$ docker-machine ssh <instance name> "<command>"
```

3. We saw how to configure our Docker Client to target the Docker Engine on our virtual instance:

```
$ eval $(docker-machine env local-vm-1)
```

and to reset it again with:

```
$ eval $(docker-machine env -u)
```

4. We turned our vanilla Docker instance into a single-node swarm cluster:

```
$ docker swarm init --advertise-addr <IP address of instance>
```

5. Having created a production version of our docker-compose.yml called docker-stack.yml, we deployed our application on the swarm as a stack using:

```
$ docker stack deploy -c docker-stack.yml myapp
```

6. We saw how to list the services in our stack with:

```
$ docker stack services myapp
```

or list all services on the swarm with:

```
$ docker service ls
```

7. We saw how to deploy an updated version of the app:

```
$ docker stack deploy -c docker-stack.yml myapp
```

8. We scaled up our web service by running multiple containers, utilizing Swarm's built-in load balancing:

```
$ docker service scale myapp_web=<n>
```

Not too shabby.

Now that we've started to get a feel for Docker Machine and Swarm, and have seen how to deploy and scale our application, it's time to move into the big leagues. In the next chapter, we'll finally move off our local machine and into the big, wide world that is the cloud.

## CHAPTER 14

Deploying to the Cloud

The cloud: our final frontier. We've already seen how to deploy to a local Swarm cluster (albeit with only a single node). In this chapter, we take this a step further and create infrastructure running in the cloud. We'll start by creating a cluster on DigitalOcean, and then see how similar this is to creating a cluster on Amazon Web Services (AWS).

By the end of this chapter, we'll have our application deployed and running in both DigitalOcean and AWS. Although our cloud deployment won't be production-grade, you'll have gained some valuable experience and started to get a feel for some of the real-world considerations at play.

Note that, as the cloud services we use in this chapter aren't free, some (small) costs are associated with running the application. However, assuming you're diligent and clean up or stop the resources when we're done, the costs will be neglible—measured in the pennies.

Creating a DigitalOcean Cluster

Before we can deploy our app to the cloud, we need cloud-based instances on which to deploy it. We're going to start by creating a Docker swarm on DigitalOcean. The prices[1] are very modest: $0.007 per hour for the smallest, standard *Droplet*—their term for an instance. In real terms, a three-node cluster running for 48 hours will cost $1.

To follow along, you'll need your own DigitalOcean account. Go to the DigitalOcean homepage and complete the sign-up form.[2] You'll need to enter your credit card details, since there is a charge for using their cloud resources.

---

1. https://www.digitalocean.com/pricing/
2. https://www.digitalocean.com

Once you've created an account, you'll need to generate an API token so that you can set up infrastructure from the command line. Log in and navigate to the API tokens page and press the "Generate New Token" button.[3] Give your token a name (for example, docker-for-rails-developers) with read/write access and then copy the generated token. I recommend you set this in your terminal as an environment variable DIGITAL_OCEAN_TOKEN for use with the following commands. On Linux or Mac, you can do this with a line:

export DIGITAL_OCEAN_TOKEN=<your token>

Put this in your .bash_rc file or equivalent, and remember to source the file now so that it's available in your current terminal session. Windows PowerShell has a similar approach.[4]

With our account set up, let's create our first cloud instance. We'll use the docker-machine create command like in the previous chapter, but specify the digitalocean driver rather than virtualbox:

```
$ docker-machine create \
  --driver digitalocean \
  --digitalocean-access-token $DIGITAL_OCEAN_TOKEN \
  --digitalocean-region lon1 \
  do-manager-1
Running pre-create checks...
Creating machine...
(do-manager-1) Creating SSH key...
(do-manager-1) Creating Digital Ocean droplet...
(do-manager-1) Waiting for IP address to be assigned to the Droplet...
Waiting for machine to be running, this may take a few minutes...
Detecting operating system of created instance...
Waiting for SSH to be available...
Detecting the provisioner...
Provisioning with ubuntu(systemd)...
Installing Docker...
Copying certs to the local machine directory...
Copying certs to the remote machine...
Setting Docker configuration on the remote daemon...
Checking connection to Docker...
Docker is up and running!
To see how to connect your Docker Client to the Docker Engine running on
this virtual machine, run: docker-machine env do-manager-1
```

---

3. https://cloud.digitalocean.com/settings/api/tokens
4. https://docs.microsoft.com/en-us/powershell/module/microsoft.powershell.core/about/about_environment_variables?view=powershell-6#changing-environment-variables

Each driver has its own set of custom configuration options.[5] We need to use the --digtialocean-access-token so docker-machine has permission to access and create instances in our account. I've also chosen a region in London (--digitalocean-region lon1) to be close to where I'm located—you can pick a region close to you from the list of regions offered by DigitalOcean.[6]

We've called the new instance do-manager-1, as we're going to use it to act as the manager for our Swarm cluster. You can see that it's now listed if we run:

```
$ docker-machine ls
NAME         ACTIVE DRIVER     STATE   URL        SWARM DOCKER    ERRORS
do-manage… -         digitaloc… Running tcp://46…       v18.09.1
local-vm-1 *          virtualbox Running tcp://19…       v18.09.1
```

Just like with our local VirtualBox instance, we can SSH onto the instance by running docker-machine ssh <instance name>:

```
$ docker-machine ssh do-manager-1
Welcome to Ubuntu 16.04.5 LTS (GNU/Linux 4.4.0-141-generic x86_64)

 * Documentation:  https://help.ubuntu.com
 * Management:     https://landscape.canonical.com
 * Support:        https://ubuntu.com/advantage

  Get cloud support with Ubuntu Advantage Cloud Guest:
    http://www.ubuntu.com/business/services/cloud

18 packages can be updated.
15 updates are security updates.
```

While we're logged in, let's initialize the instance as the swarm manager. To do this, we need to know the instance's internal IP address, which we can find by running:

```
# ifconfig eth0
eth0      Link encap:Ethernet  HWaddr 3a:87:d5:2e:22:9a
          inet addr:46.101.90.10  Bcast:46.101.95.255  Mask:255.255.240.0
          inet6 addr: fe80::3887:d5ff:fe2e:229a/64 Scope:Link
          UP BROADCAST RUNNING MULTICAST  MTU:1500  Metric:1
          RX packets:5519 errors:0 dropped:0 overruns:0 frame:0
          TX packets:3666 errors:0 dropped:0 overruns:0 carrier:0
          collisions:0 txqueuelen:1000
          RX bytes:77351515 (77.3 MB)  TX bytes:359679 (359.6 KB)
```

The IP address is listed on the second line as the inet addr value, which for me is 46.101.90.10, but for you this will differ. Now we can initialize the instance as the swarm manager:

---

5.   https://docs.docker.com/machine/drivers/digital-ocean/#options

6.   https://developers.digitalocean.com/documentation/v2/#regions

```
root@do-manager-1:~# docker swarm init --advertise-addr 46.101.90.10
Swarm initialized: current node (e2gaylk0nnr1geabo40cn3uf9) is now a manager
```

To add a worker to this swarm, run the following command:

```
    docker swarm join --token SWMTKN-1-0axry1rp0wxy6u48t4epiml4mubf9qy2y2o2f
dmq1u7n2vnj08-aoqoyn55bypasn82emb3sae27 46.101.90.10:2377
```

To add a manager to this swarm, run 'docker swarm join-token manager' and
follow the instructions.

Now that we've set up our swarm manager instance, we can exit from the box:

```
root@do-manager-1:~# exit
logout
```

For redundancy and resiliency in production environments, you'd typically
run your containers on a cluster with multiple instances. This way, if a single
node went down, the containers lost can be started up again on the remaining
instances. We're going to have a three-node cluster. To achieve this, let's
create two *worker* instances as follows:

```
$ docker-machine create \
  --driver digitalocean \
  --digitalocean-access-token $DIGITAL_OCEAN_TOKEN \
  --digitalocean-region lon1 \
  do-worker-1
Running pre-create checks...
Creating machine...
«...»
Docker is up and running!
To see how to connect your Docker Client to the Docker Engine running on
this virtual machine, run: docker-machine env do-worker-1
```

```
$ docker-machine create \
  --driver digitalocean \
  --digitalocean-access-token $DIGITAL_OCEAN_TOKEN \
  --digitalocean-region lon1 \
  do-worker-2
Running pre-create checks...
Creating machine...
«...»
Docker is up and running!
To see how to connect your Docker Client to the Docker Engine running on
this virtual machine, run: docker-machine env do-worker-2
```

We've now created two more machines in our DigitalOcean account, as we
can verify by running:

```
$ docker-machine ls
NAME            ACTIVE  DRIVER     STATE    URL         SWARM DOCKER   ERRORS
do-manager-1    -       digitaloc… Running  tcp://46…          v18.09.1
do-worker-1     -       digitaloc… Running  tcp://13…          v18.09.1
do-worker-2     -       digitaloc… Running  tcp://14…          v18.09.1
local-vm-1      *       virtualbox Running  tcp://19…          v18.09.1
```

However, at present, these two new instances aren't part of our Swarm cluster. When we initialized our swarm, the output provided the following instructions for adding workers:

```
To add a worker to this swarm, run the following command:

    docker swarm join --token SWMTKN-1-0axry1rp0wxy6u48t4epiml4mubf9qy2y2o2f
dmq1u7n2vnj08-aoqoyn55bypasn82emb3sae27 46.101.90.10:2377
```

Let's make our worker instances join the swarm now. For convenience, I suggest setting temporary environment variables in your terminal session for both the swarm token and the manager node's internal IP address:

```
SWARM_TOKEN=SWMTKN-1-0axry1rp0wxy6u48t4epiml4mubf9qy2y2o2fdmq1u7n2vnj08-aoq
oyn55bypasn82emb3sae27
MANAGER_INTERNAL_IP=46.101.90.10
```

Now we can make the workers join the swarm with the commands:

```
$ docker-machine ssh do-worker-1 \
  "docker swarm join --token $SWARM_TOKEN $MANAGER_INTERNAL_IP:2377"
This node joined a swarm as a worker.
```

and:

```
$ docker-machine ssh do-worker-2 \
  "docker swarm join --token $SWARM_TOKEN $MANAGER_INTERNAL_IP:2377"
This node joined a swarm as a worker.
```

If we're using a suitable scripting environment, we could have automated the creation of the worker instances and joining the swarm with a script like the following (using Bash):

```
SWARM_TOKEN=SWMTKN-1-0axry1rp0wxy6u48t4epiml4mubf9qy2y2o2fdmq1u7n2vnj08-aoq
oyn55bypasn82emb3sae27
MANAGER_INTERNAL_IP=46.101.90.10

for i in 1 2
do
  # create the node
  docker-machine create \
    --driver digitalocean \
    --digitalocean-access-token $DIGITAL_OCEAN_TOKEN \
    do-worker-$i
```

```
# join the swarm
docker-machine ssh do-worker-$i \
    "docker swarm join --token $SWARM_TOKEN $MANAGER_INTERNAL_IP:2377"
done
```

Deploying to Our DigitalOcean Swarm

We now have a three-node cluster in DigitalOcean. The next step is to deploy our app onto it. With Swarm, we use the same process whether we're deploying to a one-node cluster (as we did in the previous chapter), a three-node cluster (as we're about to do), or even a twenty-node cluster.

We start by configuring our Docker CLI to point to one of the manager nodes in the swarm (it's possible to have more than one manager). We can do this with docker-machine by setting the environment variables for the manager node:

```
$ eval $(docker-machine env do-manager-1)
```

Then, deploying our application is just a matter of running the docker stack deploy command. Let's do this now:

```
$ docker stack deploy -c docker-stack.yml myapp
Creating network myapp_default
Creating service myapp_db-migrator
Creating service myapp_web
Creating service myapp_redis
Creating service myapp_database
```

With our app deployed, we can see our services running on the Swarm cluster (although it may take a moment for them to all start):

```
$ docker service ls
ID    NAME               MODE   REP…  IMAGE                 PORTS
tj…   myapp_database     rep…   0/1   postgres:latest
zy…   myapp_db-migrator  rep…   0/1   robisenberg/myapp_w…
sx…   myapp_redis        rep…   0/1   redis:latest
vo…   myapp_web          rep…   0/1   robisenberg/myapp_w…  *:80->3000/tcp
```

We can also view the actual containers running for this stack (remember, it's possible to have more than one container running per service):

```
$ docker stack ps myapp
ID    NAME                  IMAGE     …  DESIRED…  CURRENT…  …  …
gm…   myapp_database.1      postgr…   …  Running   Prepari…
g8…   myapp_redis.1         redis:…   …  Running   Startin…
xx…   myapp_web.1           robise…   …  Running   Prepari…
kh…   myapp_db-migrator…    robise…   …  Running   Prepari…
```

That's it. Our app is live on the Swarm cluster. Let's visit http://any of nodes ips/welcome—you should see the hit counter. Also navigate to http://any of nodes ips/users to see that the User scaffold is working too.

If you're wondering how our database exists, that's thanks to our database service's Postgres image, which automatically creates the default database, as specified by the POSTGRES_DB environment variable we set.[7] The database has also been migrated thanks to our handy database-migrator service we added on page 163.

Visualizing Containers

As we've discussed, Swarm's orchestrator schedules containers (or more strictly, *tasks* to run containers) on whichever nodes it sees fit. That means we don't know where a container for a service will end up running.

For educational purposes, we're going to use a new "visualizer" tool that provides a web interface for seeing the nodes in our clusters, and the containers running on them; Docker provides a handy image for this. You wouldn't typically run the visualizer in production, but it will give us a feel for how containers are scheduled across the cluster.

Let's add a visualizer service to our docker-stack.yml file:

```
Line 1  visualizer:
     2    image: dockersamples/visualizer:stable
     3    ports:
     4      - "8080:8080"
     5    volumes:
     6      - "/var/run/docker.sock:/var/run/docker.sock"
     7    deploy:
     8      placement:
     9        constraints: [node.role == manager]
```

In order to view the web interface, we need to expose a port publicly. Internally, the visualizer runs on port 8080. Since nothing else in our cluster runs on this port, we've chosen to use it as the public port we expose (lines 3–4).

The visualizer relies on having access to a file called /var/run/docker.sock, which is available on the Dockerhost. We mount it into the container as a volume (line 6).

---

7.   https://hub.docker.com/_/postgres/

For the Curious: '/var/run/docker.sock'

The /var/run/docker.sock file is a socket created by the Docker daemon to allow other processes to communicate with it via a (mostly) RESTful API.[8] We can use curl to try it out—for example:

```
$ SOCKET=/var/run/docker.sock
$ ENDPOINT=http:/v1.37/containers/json
$ docker-machine ssh do-manager-1 \
    "curl --unix-socket $SOCKET $ENDPOINT"
```

You should see JSON output listing the various containers.

See the API documentation[9] and version history[10] for further details.

Next come lines 7–9. We haven't seen the deploy attribute for a service before.[11] Swarm uses attributes under this to specify various deployment-related configuration options. Here we specify what's known as a *placement constraint*:[12]

```
[node.role == manager]
```

This says, "Only deploy this service to nodes acting as a swarm manager." This is necessary because only a swarm manager will have the full information about the swarm that the visualizer needs to display.

OK, let's deploy the new visualizer service to our swarm:

```
$ docker stack deploy -c docker-stack.yml myapp
Updating service myapp_database (id: tjlxqvm3vxop9flor3u4q21y2)
Creating service myapp_visualizer
Updating service myapp_db-migrator (id: zy14mg5nosigzi9i0ysr2f51y)
Updating service myapp_web (id: vo89apdhl4y0sfobb47ly8ctp)
Updating service myapp_redis (id: sxum5csqxwcujgy0g7418fv9y)
```

Wait until the visualizer is running—the following command will show replicas "1/1" for the visualizer service when it is:

```
$ docker stack services myapp
ID    NAME              MODE   REP…  IMAGE                   PORTS
sx…   myapp_redis       rep…   1/1   redis:latest
tj…   myapp_database    rep…   1/1   postgres:latest
vo…   myapp_web         rep…   1/1   robisenberg/myapp_w…    *:80->3000/tcp
za…   myapp_visualizer  rep…   0/1   dockersamples/visua…    *:8080->8080/…
zy…   myapp_db-migrator rep…   0/1   robisenberg/myapp_w…
```

---

8.   https://docs.docker.com/develop/sdk/examples/

9.   https://docs.docker.com/engine/api/v1.37/

10. https://docs.docker.com/engine/api/version-history/

11. https://docs.docker.com/compose/compose-file/#deploy

12. https://docs.docker.com/engine/reference/commandline/service_create/#specify-service-constraints---constraint

Now we can access the web interface for the visualizer on any IP address in our swarm on port 8080. Once again, to get the IPs for our DigitalOcean nodes, you can run:

```
$ docker-machine ls
NAME            ...  ...  ...  URL                             ...  ...  ...
do-manager-1    *    ...  ...  tcp://46.101.90.10:2376         ...
do-worker-1     -    ...  ...  tcp://139.59.180.203:2376       ...
do-worker-2     -    ...  ...  tcp://142.93.32.124:2376        ...
local-vm-1      -    ...  ...  tcp://192.168.99.100:2376       ...
```

For example, I can visit http://139.59.180.203:8080 (your IP address will differ). You should see something similar to the following image:

We see three columns: one for each of our nodes. You can see that there's one container running for each of our services, with the containers spread across the cluster. The visualizer service is running on our manager node—thanks to our placement constraint.

Keep this window open, as it will be useful to see things change as we...

Scale Up the Web Service

Currently, we have a single container (or replica) of each service running on our swarm. However, with Swarm, we can scale up services to meet real or anticipated demand. Here we're talking about horizontally scaling your app—running multiple containers for a service, each of which can handle a certain amount of load.

Ready to try this out? Let's scale our web service up to run three containers; watch what happens in the visualizer as you run the following command:

```
$ docker service scale myapp_web=3
myapp_web scaled to 3
overall progress: 3 out of 3 tasks
1/3: running   [==================================================>]
2/3: running   [==================================================>]
3/3: running   [==================================================>]
verify: Service converged
```

You should see the visualizer updating in real time as containers are launched and move into the "running" state. When the command has completed, you'll see there are now three web containers. Notice that they are running across different nodes in the swarm, as shown in the following figure:

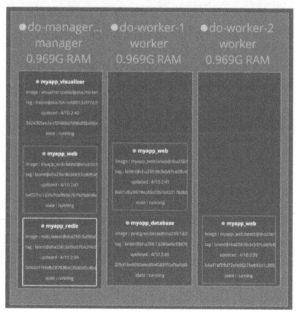

If you weren't running the visualizer, you could verify *how many* containers are running for each service with:

```
$ docker stack services myapp
ID    NAME                MODE   REP… IMAGE                  PORTS
sx…   myapp_redis         rep…   1/1  redis:latest
tj…   myapp_database      rep…   1/1  postgres:latest
vo…   myapp_web           rep…   3/3  robisenberg/myapp_w…   *:80->3000/tcp
za…   myapp_visualizer    rep…   1/1  dockersamples/visua…   *:8080->8080/…
zy…   myapp_db-migrator   rep…   0/1  robisenberg/myapp_w…
```

and see *where* they're running by issuing the command:

```
$ docker stack ps myapp
ID    NAME                   IMAGE     …  DESIRED…  CURRENT…  …  …
92…   myapp_visualizer.1     docker…   …  Running   Running…
gm…   myapp_database.1       postgr…   …  Running   Running…
g8…   myapp_redis.1          redis:…   …  Running   Running…
xx…   myapp_web.1            robise…   …  Running   Running…
kh…   myapp_db-migrator…     robise…   …  Shutdown  Complet…
uz…   myapp_web.2            robise…   …  Running   Running…
hy…   myapp_web.3            robise…   …  Running   Running…
```

To scale a service down, you use the same command as before, but specify a lower number of replicas than are currently running. For example, to scale back to a single web container, we can run:

```
$ docker service scale myapp_web=1
```

Once again, in the visualizer, you should see only a single web container.

Although we can scale a service via the docker service scale command, sometimes we want to specify this at *deploy time*. In our docker-stack.yml file, we can specify the number of containers to run for a service with the replicas attribute under deploy.

Let's modify our docker-stack.yml to make our web service start two containers when it's deployed:

```
web:
  image: robisenberg/myapp_web:prod
  ports:
    - "80:3000"
  env_file:
    - .env/production/database
    - .env/production/web
➤ deploy:
➤   replicas: 2
```

Let's see this in practice. When we deploy the app:

```
$ docker stack deploy -c docker-stack.yml myapp
Updating service myapp_database (id: tjlxqvm3vxop9flor3u4q21y2)
Updating service myapp_visualizer (id: zame53zwvvmmm70m6njrf0zd2)
Updating service myapp_db-migrator (id: zy14mg5nosigzi9i0ysr2f51y)
Updating service myapp_web (id: vo89apdhl4y0sfobb47ly8ctp)
Updating service myapp_redis (id: sxum5csqxwcujgy0g7418fv9y)
```

we should now see our two web containers running in the visualizer.

Deploying to AWS Instead of DigitalOcean

In this chapter, we've created a three-node Swarm cluster running on DigitalOcean. However, you may be thinking, "That's all very well, but what about deploying to (insert your cloud provider of choice)?" Good question.

Before we close out the chapter, we're going to see what it would take to deploy our app to a second cloud provider: AWS. The process is very similar to that for DigitalOcean; there are just two or three key differences.

Here are the steps:

1. Sign up for an AWS account if you don't already have one, and set the AWS environment variables:

    ```
    export AWS_ACCESS_KEY_ID=<your access key id>
    export AWS_SECRET_ACCESS_KEY=<your secret access key>
    export AWS_DEFAULT_REGION=<your default region>
    ```

2. Create the manager instance:

    ```
    $ docker-machine create \
    >       --driver amazonec2 \
    >       --amazonec2-open-port 80 \
    >       --amazonec2-open-port 8080 \
    >       --amazonec2-region eu-west-2 \
    >       aws-manager-1
    ```

    Note that we use the AWS-specific --amazonec2-open-port option to open up the firewall to allow us to hit ports 80 (for web) and 8080 (for visualizer).

3. Get the manager's internal IP address as before, using:

    ```
    $ docker-machine ssh aws-manager-1 "ifconfig eth0"
    ```

4. Add the user to the docker group:

    ```
    $ docker-machine ssh aws-manager-1 \
        'sudo usermod -a -G docker $USER'
    ```

    With DigitalOcean, docker-machine's SSH session is configured to connect as the root user. However, with the AWS driver, we connect via SSH as the ubuntu, non-root user. In order to have permissions to run Docker commands, we add the ubuntu user to the docker group.[13]

5. Initialize the swarm:

    ```
    $ docker-machine ssh aws-manager-1 \
        "docker swarm init --advertise-addr 172.31.29.132"
    ```

---

13. https://docs.docker.com/install/linux/linux-postinstall/#manage-docker-as-a-non-root-user

Capture the swarm token that will be given in the output.

6. Create two instances and connect them to the swarm:

```
SWARM_TOKEN=SWMTKN-1-3nzypy20thm9zd1whfsyu4kcmhxfnyo6hbivrgbec5yyz2o9yq-2
zvdcauxzl1ncs75oe8775qdg
for i in 1 2
do
  # create the node
  docker-machine create \
    --driver amazonec2 \
    --amazonec2-open-port 80 \
    --amazonec2-region eu-west-2 \
    aws-worker-$i

  # add ubuntu user to `docker` group
  docker-machine ssh aws-worker-$i \
    'sudo usermod -a -G docker $USER'

  # join the swarm
  docker-machine ssh aws-worker-$i \
    "docker swarm join --token $SWARM_TOKEN 172.31.29.132:2377"
done
```

7. Point our CLI to the manager:

```
eval $(docker-machine env aws-manager-1)
```

8. Update security group to allow swarm ports.

Docker's docs say that Swarm needs the following ports to be open:[14]

- TCP port 2377 for cluster management communications

- TCP and UDP port 7946 for communication among nodes

- UDP port 4789 for overlay network traffic

With DigitalOcean, these ports were open by default. However, with AWS, it's a little more complicated. Docker Machine instances are added to a security group called docker-machine, which restricts incoming connections (ingress) to a small number of ports that don't include those listed above. For Swarm to work correctly, we must add them.

Log in to the AWS Console, and go to EC2 > security groups. Click on the docker-machine security group, then on its Inbound Rules tab. Here, click to edit the rules and add the missing rules. It's possible to automate this process using the AWS CLI.[15]

---

14. https://docs.docker.com/engine/swarm/swarm-tutorial/#open-protocols-and-ports-between-the-hosts
15. https://semaphoreci.com/community/tutorials/bootstrapping-a-docker-swarm-mode-cluster

9. Deploy the app:

```
$ docker stack deploy -c docker-stack.yml myapp
```

10. You should now be able to reach the app by visiting http://ip address of a node/welcome. You can list the node IPs by doing:

```
$ docker-machine ls
```

Remember to Turn Out the Lights

When you're done trying things out in this chapter, remember to stop or delete your cloud instances to avoid continued charges.

To stop your instances, you can run:

```
$ docker-machine stop <instance 1> <instance 2> ...
```

or to completely remove them, run:

```
$ docker-machine rm <instance 1> <instance 2> ...
```

Quick Recap

Excellent! We've been Docker Machining and Swarming like a boss. We've deployed our application to not one, but two cloud providers, creating the infrastructure we needed as we went.

To recap:

1. We covered the steps necessary to create a multinode Swarm cluster on DigitalOcean or AWS.

2. We deployed our application to the Swarm cluster by making our Docker CLI target the manager node:

```
$ eval $(docker-machine env do-manager-1)
```

and then deploying the application:

```
$ docker stack deploy -c docker-stack.yml myapp
```

3. We used the visualizer to see the placement of containers on our nodes.

4. We learned about deploy: options that can be specified in our docker-stack.yml file, including placement constraints.[16]

5. We scaled up the service using both the command:

```
$ docker service scale myapp_web=3
```

---

16. https://docs.docker.com/engine/reference/commandline/service_create/#specify-service-constraints---constraint

and by specifying the number of replicas for a service in our docker-stack.yml:

```
service:
  deploy:
    replicas: 2
```

It's sad to say, but our Docker adventures (in this book at least) are coming to an end. In the next—and final—chapter, we'll draw things to a close, and give you some helpful pointers for continuing your journey with Docker, especially when it comes to deploying to production.

CHAPTER 15

Closing Thoughts and Next Steps

Congratulations! You've made it to the end.

Let's take a moment to reflect on our journey throughout this book. We started with just the basics: what are containers and images? We saw how Docker provides packaging (images), delivery (automatic pulling of images), and an execution runtime (containers). We learned how these fundamental pieces provide a new way of thinking about software delivery.

The rest of the book has been an extended tutorial, guiding you through the process of creating, developing, and deploying a fully featured Rails app with Docker. We generated the Rails app using a container, and we created a custom image for running our Rails app, which we gradually enhanced. We introduced Docker Compose, using it to build up to a multiservice application with Redis, a database with decoupled volume for its data.

We made our Dockerized setup play nice with JavaScript, as we saw how to work with both the standard asset pipeline and webpacker, Rails' newest approach for integrating modern JavaScript front ends. We also covered how to test our app, going as far as running end-to-end tests relying on JavaScript in Chrome in both headless and non-headless mode.

However, even in Docker-land, nothing is perfect. We explored a couple of irritations you might encounter when working with Docker, and we did our best to mitigate these.

Finally, we started our journey toward production. After a quick tour of the production landscape to understand the capabilities we need and the tools available, we enhanced our app to be deployable in a production environment. We learned how to push our Docker images to a Registry, making them available for delivery to other machines. Next we introduced Swarm and used it to create our very own production-like playground on our local machine.

Finally, we took this to the next level and deployed our app to the Cloud, using a three-node cluster on both DigitalOcean and AWS, and we used this to demonstrate Swarm's scaling capabilities.

That's a heck of a lot to have achieved (especially for a book of this size!). I'll leave the choice of celebration in your capable hands, although I'd urge you to think bigger than the proverbial pat on the back.

However, although we've started our journey toward production, there's too much to cover to get to a fully resilient, CI/CD pipeline-driven, secure, scalable production environment. Hopefully, you've had a taste of the power that Docker offers, and you can see its potential and are inspired to learn more.

This short chapter is a grab bag of various things we couldn't squeeze in elsewhere. As well as planting some seeds of ideas in your mind that you'll find useful, this chapter will provide you some pointers on continuing your journey with Docker.

What Should I Learn About Next?

Great question. As you no doubt are aware, our learning never ends. The more you know, the more you realize you don't know. C'est la vie.

To help in this effort, I'm going to share my thoughts on (what I consider to be) valuable areas for further learning. For each topic, I'll provide a brief summary, but you'll have to do a bit of digging to learn more and think about how to apply these to your application. Some areas will be more or less appealing and more or less useful in your situation, so dig deeper into the areas you need, and feel free to leave what you don't.

Enjoy!

Limiting Resources

As you run more containers in your cluster, you may find the need to constrain the CPU resources and memory given to certain containers. Both Swarm[1] and Kubernetes[2] provide a way to specify limits on the resources a container is allowed.

Here's an example with Swarm that means containers for some-service will only receive a maximum of 50 MB of memory, and one tenth of a single CPU core.

---

1. https://docs.docker.com/config/containers/resource_constraints/
2. https://kubernetes.io/docs/concepts/configuration/manage-compute-resources-container/

```
services:
  some-service:
    deploy:
      resources:
        limits:
          cpus: "0.1"
          memory: 50M
```

Autoscaling

What's better than running a command to scale up a service? Running *no* commands to scale up a service. This is known as autoscaling. It involves monitoring key usage and load metrics for containers and detecting when they get close to becoming overloaded. At this point, the new containers for the service are launched to meet with additional demand. As the load dies down, this is again detected, and the service is scaled back down, freeing up more resources.

Unfortunately, Swarm does not provide built-in autoscaling, although it's possible to engineer it yourself with each node in the cluster exporting metrics (using something like cadvisor[3] to a central metric service, such as Prometheus[4]). If that sounds like too much work, you could consider one of various open source solutions, such as Orbiter.[5] Your final option is to switch to using Kubernetes[6] for your container orchestration. Although more complex, it is more fully featured and has autoscaling built in.[7]

Zero-Downtime, Blue-Green Deploys

The pinnacle of a good continuous deployment pipeline is being able to deploy updates to your app in a seamless, safe way, with no downtime or impact on users. Typically, this is achieved with *blue-green* deploys, where a second version of the application is started, and then traffic is (usually gradually) cut over to the new version of the app. The previous version of the app is kept around (at least for a while) in case a problem emerges that means you need to roll back.

Docker Swarm provides some capabilities for performing these type of rolling updates.[8] While this can be useful, unfortunately Swarm currently doesn't

---

3. https://github.com/google/cadvisor
4. https://prometheus.io
5. https://github.com/gianarb/orbiter
6. https://kubernetes.io
7. https://kubernetes.io/docs/tasks/run-application/horizontal-pod-autoscale/
8. https://docs.docker.com/engine/swarm/swarm-tutorial/rolling-update/

support *session affinity*, also known as *sticky sessions*. That is, once an updated version of your app has been deployed, any new sessions will be handled by this latest version, but any existing user sessions will continue to be serviced by the old version. This is important because the old version may be incompatible with your updated version of the app in some way, particularly if routes or database schemas have changed.

You can still achieve zero-downtime deploys with Swarm, but it will involve some extra work, typically requiring you to run a reverse proxy in front of the app that *does* provide session affinity. Zero-downtime deploys can also be achieved with Kubernetes, but this similarly involves some work.[9]

Security

It's beyond the scope of this book to teach you the ins and outs of securing your cloud-based infrastructure, but if you're building a production environment, this will be a key area to get right. Unfortunately, there's no *one-size-fits-all* approach, particularly as things can vary greatly between cloud platforms.

A good starting place is Docker's own docs on the subject.[10] Make sure you see the various pages under "Security" in the menu—there's no "Next" button at the bottom of the page. Key topics are: only using trusted images, scanning images for vulnerabilities, not running containers as root,[11] and locking down firewalls to the bare minimum ports required, plus more involved ways to lock down your Docker installation.

More Advanced Architectural Possibilities

So far we've used Swarm's built-in load-balancing capabilities to distribute incoming requests to different containers backing a given service. However, as you get more experienced, you may want to use more sophisticated setups with things like HAProxy[12] or NGINX[13] to do your own proxying and load balancing.

Not only is this possible, but you can run HAProxy or NGINX instances in containers themselves, building your own images with your config files. You can also use Docker's network primitives[14] to create different network configurations.

---

9. https://medium.com/@diegomrtnzg/redirect-your-users-to-the-same-pod-by-using-session-affinity-on-kubernetes-baebf6a1733b
10. https://docs.docker.com/engine/security/security/
11. https://docs.docker.com/engine/security/userns-remap/
12. http://www.haproxy.org
13. https://www.nginx.com
14. https://docs.docker.com/v17.09/engine/swarm/networking/

This can allow you to wall off containers from each other and control which containers can communicate with others.

Secret Management

In this book, we followed many of the twelve-factor app principles.[15] For example, we externalized our app config, making it available as environment variables.[16] However, it turns out that environment variables aren't particularly secure—they're available to the entire process, easily leaked, and violate the principle of least privilege.[17] Docker offers a more secure, built-in option called Docker secrets.[18]

Docker secrets are added to a swarm with the docker secret create command (having first targeted a swarm manager). Alternatively, you can specify secrets in your deploy file (in Compose format).[19]

Secrets are encrypted inside Swarm's data structures that store them (encryption at rest), as well as on their entire journey to reach the containers that need them (encryption in transit). They are made available to a container via an in-memory filesystem that's mounted at /run/secrets/<secret_name>. Only containers explicitly given access to a secret are able to access it.

There's even a built-in mechanism for rotating secrets,[20] which makes it more likely you'll do the Right Thing and rotate your secrets frequently.

Restarting on Failure

By default, when the process running inside a container terminates, the container is stopped. Sometimes, this behavior is exactly what we want. For example, our database-migrator service is supposed to do its job of migrating the database and then exit.

However, what about our Rails app containers running in production? If something goes wrong that causes the app to crash (for example, in the case of a memory leak), it would be nice if the containers themselves could be resilient and handle failures more gracefully. Who wants to be woken in the middle of the night to fix issues?

---

15. https://12factor.net
16. https://12factor.net/config
17. http://movingfast.io/articles/environment-variables-considered-harmful/
18. https://docs.docker.com/engine/swarm/secrets/
19. https://docs.docker.com/engine/swarm/secrets/#use-secrets-in-compose
20. https://docs.docker.com/engine/swarm/secrets/#example-rotate-a-secret

Docker allows you to define a *restart policy* that says how it should behave when the container terminates.[21] By setting this to on-failure:

```
deploy:
  restart_policy:
    condition: on-failure
```

Swarm will now automatically restart our Rails app were it to crash. Here's a good article with more details.[22]

Multi-stage Builds

Large Docker images are slower to push and pull. As you become more experienced with Docker, you'll want to find ways to make your images. Since version 17.05, Docker has had a feature called multi-stage builds[23]—this lets you use multiple FROM statements in a single Dockerfile. Each new FROM is considered a new stage, and starts as a fresh new image. However, the COPY instruction has been enhanced to let you copy files from *earlier stages*.

The most obvious use case is where you need a lot of development tools that produce a final artifact. Think of a static site generator like Jekyll[24] or Middleman[25]—you need various tools to develop and generate the site, but once the static files are generated, they're the only thing needed to run the site. Multi-stage builds let you create an initial stage that generates the site, and a separate, final stage that copies those files into a clean web server image. The same goes for compiled languages like Go where, typically, the only thing you need to include in your final image is the compiled binary.

In the case of our Rails app, a quick win could be copying the precompiled assets into a final image, avoiding the need for all the JavaScript dependencies. There are other ways to save space if you think creatively and see what other people are doing.

Docker Stats

Often, especially in production, it's useful to have a quick way to find out metrics about the resources being used. The Docker docs[26] provide some useful information on various metrics you can check out.

---

21. https://docs.docker.com/config/containers/start-containers-automatically/#use-a-restart-policy
22. https://blog.codeship.com/ensuring-containers-are-always-running-with-dockers-restart-policy/
23. https://docs.docker.com/develop/develop-images/multistage-build/
24. https://jekyllrb.com
25. https://middlemanapp.com
26. https://docs.docker.com/config/containers/runmetrics/

One of the simplest and most useful is the docker stats command. This provides various metrics, including CPU, memory usage, and network IO, which can be helpful for monitoring or debugging containers in production.

Here's an example from Docker's docs:[27]

```
$ docker stats redis1 redis2
```

```
CONTAINER  CPU %  MEM USAGE / LIMIT  MEM %  NET I/O           BLOCK I/O
redis1     0.07%  796 KB / 64 MB     1.21%  788 B / 648 B     ...
redis2     0.07%  2.746 MB / 64 MB   4.29%  1.266 KB / 648 B  ...
```

Sharing Config Between Compose Files

We're currently maintaining two files in Compose format: docker-compose.yml and docker-compose.prod.yml. You may find that, as you develop your app, you notice quite a lot of duplication between the Compose files for different environments.

Compose provides a mechanism that lets you extract the commonalities.[28] It does this by allowing you to specify multiple Compose files:

```
docker-compose -f <file1> -f <file2> ... -f <fileN> up -d
```

Compose merges the config from the specified files, with config in later files taking precedence over config in earlier files.

As always, keeping or eliminating duplication both have trade-offs. On the plus side, extracting the duplication to a common file makes the *differences* between your environments clearer—these are the parts you will have to specify for an environment beyond the common base. It also (potentially) makes it (marginally) quicker to update the config for both sets of services. On the downside, you have to piece together the definitions from multiple files to understand your app as a whole. As you can probably tell, this is an instance where I think the benefits of keeping the duplication outweigh our programmer instinct to keep things DRY.[29]

However, it's worth knowing you have this option at your disposal should you need it. For example, this can also be put to use to keep common, one-off container admin tasks in a separate Compose file, rather than the same one as the application.

---

27. https://docs.docker.com/config/containers/runmetrics/#docker-stats
28. https://docs.docker.com/compose/extends/
29. https://en.wikipedia.org/wiki/Don%27t_repeat_yourself

Database Resiliency

Ensuring we back up our production database regularly is critical to ensure we can recover in case of error; it's possible to back up a database by running the normal database dump command inside a container. However, what's slightly trickier is how to make this happen automatically in production.

There are a number of different ways to handle this:

- *Platform-specific.* Some container platforms allow you to schedule containers (for example, Amazon ECS scheduled tasks).[30] Using these schedulers, you can run containers to back up the database at regular intervals. Additionally, platforms may offer backup capabilities; for example, Amazon Elastic Block Store (Amazon EBS) volumes provide automated incremental snapshotting capabilities.[31] This can be a low-hassle, reliable approach to maintaining backups.

- *Cron running on the Dockerhost.* There's nothing stopping you from setting up cron or a similar scheduler on your Dockerhost that triggers a container (or noncontainerized script) for backing up the database. Some people like this approach, particularly because of its simplicity. However, the downside is the risk that your Dockerhost becomes a special snowflake that's harder to maintain. Your database backup mechanism is living outside of your containerization, so you lose all the benefits that brings.

- *Use third-party tools.* For example, Barman for Postgres.[32]

Containers on Autopilot

There's a broader approach that's beginning to emerge known as *the autopilot pattern.*[33] This involves baking standard operational tasks (such as scaling and resiliency) directly into your containerized services themselves.

Rather than maintaining this operational logic spread externally with schedulers and separate task-based containers, your app containers have the smarts to perform their own life-cycle management. For example, imagine launching a Postgres container configured to check if its database was populated, and if it finds that it wasn't, goes and fetches and restores the latest backup. Done well, maintenance and resiliency become automatic.

---

30. https://docs.aws.amazon.com/AmazonECS/latest/developerguide/scheduled_tasks.html
31. https://docs.aws.amazon.com/AWSEC2/latest/UserGuide/snapshot-lifecycle.html
32. https://www.pgbarman.org/about/
33. http://autopilotpattern.io

Joyent[34] has been championing this approach, with several[35] compelling articles[36] on the subject. It also provides an open source tool called ContainerPilot[37] to help with the coordination of life-cycle events. Alternatively, you can roll your own solution. I suspect we'll see more in this space over time.

Database Replication and High Availability

To replicate your database, you typically need to rely on the built-in capabilities of your database (rather than a super naive approach of trying to use a shared filesystem).

Postgres offers many different options for clustering.[38] Rather than reinventing the wheel, however, you can leverage the work that others have done in this area—for example:

- Patroni[39]
- Barman[40]
- Crunchy[41]

You'll find similar work has been done for clustering and replicating other databases too.

---

34. https://www.joyent.com
35. https://www.joyent.com/blog/app-centric-micro-orchestration
36. https://www.joyent.com/blog/persistent-storage-patterns
37. https://www.joyent.com/containerpilot
38. https://wiki.postgresql.org/wiki/Replication,_Clustering,_and_Connection_Pooling
39. https://github.com/zalando/patroni
40. https://hub.docker.com/r/postdock/barman/
41. http://info.crunchydata.com/blog/an-easy-recipe-for-creating-a-postgresql-cluster-with-docker-swarm

APPENDIX 1

Platform Differences

Although Docker strives for complete platform independence, there's at least one notable way in which the platforms differ. Let's take a quick look and see what the deal is.

File Ownership and Permissions

There are some subtle differences when it comes to how file ownership and permissions are handled on the different Docker platforms (Mac, Linux, and Windows). These differences can cause a slight issue when you write files to a mounted volume from inside a container.

The issue stems from the fact that there are usually different user accounts being used inside and outside a container. Typically, you use your normal user account on your machine, but inside a container, the default user is the container's root account. This means that files created inside the container are owned by that root user.

When you exit the container, the question is, will you be able to modify these files that are owned by root? The answer is slightly different for each platform.

On Docker for Windows, files created inside the container have file permissions that allow them to be modified by anyone (the equivalent of Unix file permission 777). This means there's no issue with using and modifying the files outside the container.

Docker for Mac uses its own separate file-sharing system called osxfs.[1] It does some trickery[2] to make it seem like the mounted files are owned by whichever

---

1. https://docs.docker.com/docker-for-mac/osxfs/
2. https://stackoverflow.com/questions/43097341/docker-on-macosx-does-not-translate-file-ownership-correctly-in-volumes

user in the container accesses/creates them. However, in reality, the files on your local filesystem are owned by whichever macOS user account owns them. In practice, this means that mounted files are readable and writeable both inside and outside the container without having to modify file ownership.

On Linux, there is no magic or trickery to insulate you from the file ownership differences between inside a container and outside the container on your local machine. If files inside the container are owned by root, then outside the container they are still owned by root. We always have to do something to ensure files generated inside our container are editable by us outside the container.

We can take one of two approaches:

1. Use the --user "$(id -u):$(id -g)" option, which runs the command with your local user's ID and group ID—for example:

   ```
   $ docker-compose exec --user "$(id -u):$(id -g)" web \
       bin/rails generate controller welcome index
   ```

2. chown the files by running the following from your Rails root:

   ```
   $ sudo chown <your_user>:<your_group> -R .
   ```

For me, the latter seems the most straightforward, and this is the one I suggest throughout the book. To save on typing, you could even create a Rake task or shell command alias.

Finding Images to Use

Throughout the book, we use a number of different *known* images. You may be wondering how you'd find images to use if you had to do this yourself. By the time you finish this book, it's important for you to be self-sufficient and able to figure things out for yourself, so let's delve into this now.

Imagine we want to run a Postgres database, and we need to find an image that provides it. There are two ways you can go about finding images: using Docker Hub—Docker's online service for storing images—or Docker's command-line interface (CLI.) Let's look at both in turn.

Using Docker Hub

You may remember we've already visited Docker Hub to create our account there in Chapter 1. Let's visit it again and see how we can use it to find images.

Go to hub.docker.com in your browser. Type "postgres" in the main search box and press Enter. You should see a results screen that looks like the following:

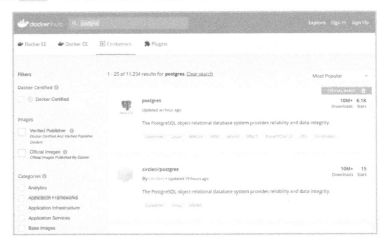

The top result should be the official Postgres image. Click that, and it will take you to the following information page:[1]

The really great thing about these Docker Hub repository pages is that image providers—Postgres, in this case—can, and usually do, provide detailed information on how to use the image.

I recommend sticking with Docker Official Images[2] wherever possible since these are vetted for security vulnerabilities by Docker, and they commit to applying security updates in a timely manner. Outside of these, you have no guarantees about what software an image may be running or how quickly the image is updated.

Using the Docker CLI

The other way to find images is by using the Docker CLI. For example, to find Postgres-related images, you would use the following command:

```
$ docker search postgres
```

If you run this now, you'll see output similar to the following:

```
NAME                      DESCRIPTION             STARS  OFFICIAL  AUTOMATED
postgres                  The PostgreSQL object-r...  3828   [OK]
kiasaki/alpine-postgres   PostgreSQL docker image...  33               [OK]
nornagon/postgres                                     10               [OK]
macadmins/postgres        Postgres that accepts r...  8                [OK]
«...»
```

---

1. https://hub.docker.com/_/postgres/
2. https://docs.docker.com/docker-hub/official_images/

As you can see, the official postgres image is shown first, along with several others. Images are shown in order of the number of times the image has been "starred," which is an indication of how popular the image is. The output also has a column to tell us whether this is an official (in other words, Docker-approved) image or not. Again, stick with official images from Docker Hub wherever possible.

Index

Thank you!

How did you enjoy this book? Please let us know. Take a moment and email us at support@pragprog.com with your feedback. Tell us your story and you could win free ebooks. Please use the subject line "Book Feedback."

Ready for your next great Pragmatic Bookshelf book? Come on over to https://pragprog.com and use the coupon code BUYANOTHER2019 to save 30% on your next ebook.

Void where prohibited, restricted, or otherwise unwelcome. Do not use ebooks near water. If rash persists, see a doctor. Doesn't apply to *The Pragmatic Programmer* ebook because it's older than the Pragmatic Bookshelf itself. Side effects may include increased knowledge and skill, increased marketability, and deep satisfaction. Increase dosage regularly.

And thank you for your continued support,

Andy Hunt, Publisher

SAVE 30%!
Use coupon code
BUYANOTHER2019

More Rails

The classic introduction to Rails, for you and everyone new on your team, and the best of the best for testing on Rails.

Agile Web Development with Rails 5.1

Learn Rails the way the Rails core team recommends it, along with the tens of thousands of developers who have used this broad, far-reaching tutorial and reference. If you're new to Rails, you'll get step-by-step guidance. If you're an experienced developer, get the comprehensive, insider information you need for the latest version of Ruby on Rails. The new edition of this award-winning classic is completely updated for Rails 5.1 and Ruby 2.4, with information on system testing, Webpack, and advanced JavaScript.

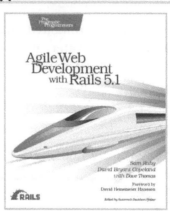

Sam Ruby and David Bryant Copeland
(494 pages) ISBN: 9781680502510. $57.95
https://pragprog.com/book/rails51

Rails 5 Test Prescriptions

Does your Rails code suffer from bloat, brittleness, or inaccuracy? Cure these problems with the regular application of test-driven development. You'll use Rails 5.2, Minitest 5, and RSpec 3.7, as well as popular testing libraries such as factory_bot and Cucumber. Updates include Rails 5.2 system tests and Webpack integration. Do what the doctor ordered to make your applications feel all better. Side effects may include better code, fewer bugs, and happier developers.

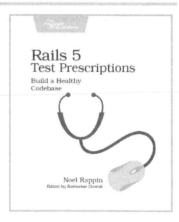

Noel Rappin
(404 pages) ISBN: 9781680502503. $47.95
https://pragprog.com/book/nrtest3

Level Up

From daily programming to architecture and design, level up your skills starting today.

Exercises for Programmers

When you write software, you need to be at the top of your game. Great programmers practice to keep their skills sharp. Get sharp and stay sharp with more than fifty practice exercises rooted in real-world scenarios. If you're a new programmer, these challenges will help you learn what you need to break into the field, and if you're a seasoned pro, you can use these exercises to learn that hot new language for your next gig.

Brian P. Hogan
(118 pages) ISBN: 9781680501223. $24
https://pragprog.com/book/bhwb

A Common-Sense Guide to Data Structures and Algorithms

If you last saw algorithms in a university course or at a job interview, you're missing out on what they can do for your code. Learn different sorting and searching techniques, and when to use each. Find out how to use recursion effectively. Discover structures for specialized applications, such as trees and graphs. Use Big O notation to decide which algorithms are best for your production environment. Beginners will learn how to use these techniques from the start, and experienced developers will rediscover approaches they may have forgotten.

Jay Wengrow
(220 pages) ISBN: 9781680502442. $45.95
https://pragprog.com/book/jwdsal

Pragmatic Programming

We'll show you how to be more pragmatic and effective, for new code and old.

Your Code as a Crime Scene

Jack the Ripper and legacy codebases have more in common than you'd think. Inspired by forensic psychology methods, this book teaches you strategies to predict the future of your codebase, assess refactoring direction, and understand how your team influences the design. With its unique blend of forensic psychology and code analysis, this book arms you with the strategies you need, no matter what programming language you use.

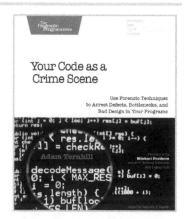

Adam Tornhill
(218 pages) ISBN: 9781680500387. $36
https://pragprog.com/book/atcrime

The Nature of Software Development

You need to get value from your software project. You need it "free, now, and perfect." We can't get you there, but we can help you get to "cheaper, sooner, and better." This book leads you from the desire for value down to the specific activities that help good Agile projects deliver better software sooner, and at a lower cost. Using simple sketches and a few words, the author invites you to follow his path of learning and understanding from a half century of software development and from his engagement with Agile methods from their very beginning.

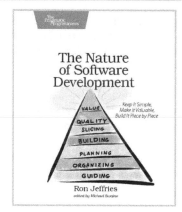

Ron Jeffries
(176 pages) ISBN: 9781941222379. $24
https://pragprog.com/book/rjnsd

The Joy of Mazes and Math

Rediscover the joy and fascinating weirdness of mazes and pure mathematics.

Mazes for Programmers

A book on mazes? Seriously?

Yes!

Not because you spend your day creating mazes, or because you particularly like solving mazes.

But because it's fun. Remember when programming used to be fun? This book takes you back to those days when you were starting to program, and you wanted to make your code do things, draw things, and solve puzzles. It's fun because it lets you explore and grow your code, and reminds you how it feels to just think.

Sometimes it feels like you live your life in a maze of twisty little passages, all alike. Now you can code your way out.

Jamis Buck
(286 pages) ISBN: 9781680500554. $38
https://pragprog.com/book/jbmaze

Good Math

Mathematics is beautiful—and it can be fun and exciting as well as practical. *Good Math* is your guide to some of the most intriguing topics from two thousand years of mathematics: from Egyptian fractions to Turing machines; from the real meaning of numbers to proof trees, group symmetry, and mechanical computation. If you've ever wondered what lay beyond the proofs you struggled to complete in high school geometry, or what limits the capabilities of the computer on your desk, this is the book for you.

Mark C. Chu-Carroll
(282 pages) ISBN: 9781937785338. $34
https://pragprog.com/book/mcmath

The Pragmatic Bookshelf

The Pragmatic Bookshelf features books written by developers for developers. The titles continue the well-known Pragmatic Programmer style and continue to garner awards and rave reviews. As development gets more and more difficult, the Pragmatic Programmers will be there with more titles and products to help you stay on top of your game.

Visit Us Online

This Book's Home Page
https://pragprog.com/book/ridocker
Source code from this book, errata, and other resources. Come give us feedback, too!

Keep Up to Date
https://pragprog.com
Join our announcement mailing list (low volume) or follow us on twitter @pragprog for new titles, sales, coupons, hot tips, and more.

New and Noteworthy
https://pragprog.com/news
Check out the latest pragmatic developments, new titles and other offerings.

Save on the eBook

Save on the eBook versions of this title. Owning the paper version of this book entitles you to purchase the electronic versions at a terrific discount.

PDFs are great for carrying around on your laptop—they are hyperlinked, have color, and are fully searchable. Most titles are also available for the iPhone and iPod touch, Amazon Kindle, and other popular e-book readers.

Buy now at *https://pragprog.com/coupon*

Contact Us

Online Orders:	*https://pragprog.com/catalog*
Customer Service:	*support@pragprog.com*
International Rights:	*translations@pragprog.com*
Academic Use:	*academic@pragprog.com*
Write for Us:	*http://write-for-us.pragprog.com*
Or Call:	+1 800-699-7764